Praise

"A singular and unforgettable take on what it is like to have your world cracked open by extreme physical disability. This book is a compelling piece of advocacy, a strike against invisibility, and an inspiration."

—Mary Roach, *New York Times* bestselling author

"Jeremy Schreiber approaches his devastating diagnosis with courage and humor—and in doing so delivers a wake-up call that urges us to rethink the way we see, or fail to see, those with disabilities."

—David Litt, *New York Times* bestselling author

"Jeremy Schreiber has written an engaging memoir about his journey with ALS, as well a clear and concise guide for those facing serious health issues, their caregivers, and just about everyone else. Filled with honesty, poignancy, passion, and humor, it will open your eyes and possibly your heart."

—Sue Monk Kidd, *New York Times* bestselling author

"You will finish this book and feel nothing but actual love for the man who wrote it. You will thank him for making you remember that every second is precious. And we are all so lucky to be alive, whether we can turn the pages of this page-turner ourselves or not."

—Augusten Burroughs, *New York Times* bestselling author

"This book reflects the extraordinary life of a truly courageous man. With humor, common sense, compassion, and without feeling sorry for himself in the least, Jeremy Schreiber takes you on a journey through the hellish trauma of ALS . . . beautifully written."

—David Crow, award-winning author of *The Pale-Faced Lie*

NEVER SAY INVISIBLE

A Memoir of Living and
Being Seen with ALS

Jeremy Schreiber

Foreword by Augusten Burroughs

SANDRA JONAS
PUBLISHING

Sandra Jonas Publishing House
PO Box 20892
Boulder, CO 80308
sandrajonaspublishing.com

Printed in the United States of America
27 26 25 24 23 22 3 4 5 6 7 8 9

Book and cover design by Sandra Jonas

Publisher's Cataloging-in-Publication Data

Names: Schreiber, Jeremy, 1979–2021, author.
Title: Never Say Invisible: A Memoir of Living and Being Seen with ALS / Jeremy Schreiber.
Description: Boulder, CO : Sandra Jonas Publishing, 2022.
Identifiers: LCCN 2022938036 | ISBN 9781954861008 (hardcover) 9781954861015 (paperback)
Subjects: LCSH: Schreiber, Jeremy, 1979-2021. | Amyotrophic lateral sclerosis — Patients —United States — Biography. | LCGFT: Autobiographies. | BISAC: BIOGRAPHY & AUTOBIOGRAPHY / Personal Memoirs.
Classification: LCC RC406.A24 S37 | DDC 616.8390092—dc23
LC record available at http://lccn.loc.gov/2022938036

All photographs are from the author's private collection.

To my parents

My love and gratitude for all that you are and all that you have done goes beyond what words can describe. I could not have asked for better parents than you.

To Melissa Simpson

My unicorn of sunshine, you make everything better.

To Todd Adest

You are my personal savior.

To the men of MDI

Men, I am Schreiber. This journey would have been painfully different if it were not for each of you. Complete.

Contents

Contents

Publisher's Note

After a long, courageous battle with ALS, Jeremy Schreiber died on October 29, 2021, while writing this book. The team at Sandra Jonas Publishing collaborated with his parents, Fred and Ronnye Schreiber, to finish and release his memoir, allowing his words to live on as a guide and inspiration to all of us. In Jeremy's honor, we will continue working together to raise awareness for this devastating disease, as well as for the millions of people struggling with disabilities.

All the stories in this book reflect his recollection of events. Some names, locations, and identifying characteristics have been changed to protect the privacy of those depicted.

The information presented is based on Jeremy's experience and should not be used for diagnosis or treatment or as a substitute for professional care.

A final note: We use the word "accessible" to mean "accessible by people who have a disability."

Foreword by Augusten Burroughs

When Jeremy Schreiber—whom I did not know—emailed me requesting a blurb for his memoir about his journey with ALS, my favorite part was that he provided two prewritten blurbs from which to choose. Not that he was pressuring me to use either one, mind you. He was being thoughtful and helpful in case I was too busy to read the book myself.

I've been asked for a lot of blurbs, but no author had ever included options.

I wrote him back and told him I would read his manuscript immediately. "You telepathically saw into my coal-filled soul and understood: *your* ALS is actually about me and *my* deep aversion to the slightest physical discomfort, which would include the extraordinary effort of typing a blurb for you."

When I wrote that last line, I did not yet know that Jeremy had to type using his eyes, one letter at a time.

I read *Never Say Invisible* and I was riveted by his story. I wrote a blurb and then we continued exchanging emails. Because it takes Jeremy a long time to write—and because he has a great deal to say—long periods of time would pass between our emails, and I sometimes worried that I'd offended him. (See the above comment about typing.) Then he'd come back with insight, wisdom, and double the dark humor.

I have physical health and full mobility and Jeremy does not.

His daily life is painful and challenging in so many ways. As the author of memoirs about the abuse and neglect I experienced as a child and my alcoholism as an adult, I've been asked thousands of times, "How did you survive that?"

I was not accustomed to being on the other end.

During the pandemic, there were periods when I felt a surreal, flat hopelessness. Then a long email from Jeremy would burst into my world. The more challenges his disease threw at him, the more ambitious he became.

In my reply to his initial email, I wrote,

> I don't have to know one more thing about you to know everything about you. You'll open the door. You'll pick up the check. You'll fix the sink. You'll change the diapers.
>
> You're the guy who sees the pregnant girl get on the subway before she sees you see her and you are already standing up to give her your seat when her eye suddenly catches yours and she's kind of shocked by how weirdly instantaneous this whole "here, take mine" thing is, but she's also grateful because she hates gravity these days.
>
> You're the guy who will take the first slice of cake, the one where all the frosting gets broken into pieces, so that everyone else can have a pretty piece. These are things you do automatically and for free. And even if you can't do all these things anymore, you would if you could, and therefore you do.

Time and knowledge have revealed that every word of that was absolutely true. I could see him immediately because he showed me who he was. Jeremy has been punched and kicked and beaten bloody by a violent, psychopathic disease, and yet he remains undefeated: chivalrous, courteous, and honorable. Always. Jeremy is Mr. Knightley.

It is true that he has lost a great deal in this life. But it is also true that he has gained something: the knowledge that he possesses not one weak fiber within his body or soul. Disease has not broken him; it has merely forged his interior steel.

Real heroes don't wear capes. Sometimes, they can't even swallow on their own.

1

Something Went Terribly Wrong

"I guess it comes down to a simple choice, really.
Get busy living or get busy dying."
—Andy Dufresne in *The Shawshank Redemption*

I LOVED TO RUN.

Every morning at five, rain or shine, I'd shoot out of my apartment at 40th Street and 2nd Avenue in Manhattan, traverse over to 3rd Avenue, up to 59th Street, past the Apple Store and the Plaza Hotel, and into the southeast corner of Central Park. From there I would make my way north until I reached the reservoir, where I would cut in. On days when I had more time, I would keep running north, wrapping around the very top of Central Park at 110th Street and back down the west side. Mile after mile of pure joy.

I was thirty-six years old with a new wife and a flourishing career in sales. I was unstoppable.

And then something went terribly wrong.

When I crossed the finish line of the Brooklyn Half Marathon in May 2016, my legs hurt. A lot. Shin splints, or at least that's what I thought. Physical therapy seemed to help, though my legs probably improved because I had stopped running. Months later, the pain persisted.

And then my right foot started behaving strangely. When I'd climb stairs or step onto a curb, it would suddenly hang straight down, lifeless, invariably causing me to trip. Still, I kept thinking that if the Tarahumara could wear handmade sandals and run hundreds of miles on dirt trails in sweltering heat, surely I'd be able to handle a pretty jog around Central Park.

But as the winter turned into spring, I developed other symptoms. Muscle cramps, muscle twitching, weakness in my hands, legs, feet, and ankles, and difficulty speaking and swallowing. And no one could tell me what was wrong.

For nine months, I went from one specialty doctor to the next in New York City (NYC), undergoing tests for everything from allergies to Zika. It wasn't until I spent a week at the Mayo Clinic in Rochester, Minnesota, to get a second—or in this case a sixth—opinion that I finally received the diagnosis.

"This is ALS," the doctor said. "No question."

Amyotrophic lateral sclerosis. Lou Gehrig's disease.

The *A* word had been nagging at the back of my mind throughout my search for answers, though I kept pushing it further back each time a new bit of information surfaced or I came across some new research. I did all I could to logic away from my greatest fear.

I couldn't do that anymore.

Tears streamed down my face. I had a hollow where my heart and stomach had been.

My parents were with me, and my wife was on the phone from NYC. The doctor sent us home that day with an envelope full of pamphlets and these parting words: "Get your accounts in order."

It was January 5, 2018. And I had just been handed a death sentence.

For the first week, I could hardly eat or sleep. If I managed to sleep at all, I would wake up forgetting that my life as I'd known it was over. For a few seconds, everything was perfect. But then I would remember, and I'd start sobbing again.

One morning, I stood in my apartment on forearm crutches, staring into the floor-length mirror in my hallway. I had a choice—climb into bed and pull the covers over my head or say "fuck it" and fight this thing head-on. On that cold January day, I told myself I was going to fight this thing with everything I had.

For sure, I didn't have time to make my way through whatever stages of grief my therapist told me I was supposed to experience. I needed to throw this life into overdrive and hurry up—but hurry up doing what? Whatever it was going to be had to happen, and fast.

Questions flooded in from everyone and everywhere. My own brain was proving to be the greatest and, quite frankly, the least helpful source.

I had mountains of information, yet it all said pretty much the same thing. There's no known cause for most cases of ALS. It can run in families, but no one in my family had had it. And there's no real way to manage the symptoms. Statistically, I had only two to five years to live, though about 10 percent survive at least ten years.

Surely not every person with ALS sat around waiting to die. I needed to find out who the pioneers were and what they were doing to beat the statistics and then build on that. All this while maintaining my now-strained marriage, holding down a job, and managing my own sanity.

ALS, also known as motor neuron disease (MND), destroys nerve cells in the brain and spinal cord that control the muscles throughout the body, including the chest muscles and diaphragm.

As my symptoms worsened and I moved from crutches to a walker and then to a wheelchair, traveling around the city became more and more difficult. Broken curbs, heavy doors, and inaccessible buildings created new obstacles for me to manage. Cabs were more challenging to get in and out of. Wide-open spaces that lacked something to grab onto were terrifying to traverse. Because nothing was "accessible" to fit my needs, my days were planned around the fewest possible steps.

It was like they had conspired to break my spirit. I had no days off, no late-night infomercials urging me to cure my ailments with a remedy bought in the next ten minutes.

I received a barrage of calls from well-wishers saying how sorry they were and offering to help in any way possible. But there was little they could do. The unfriendliness of how the world is built would now add an unwelcome layer of complexity to this uphill battle I was facing.

The Americans with Disabilities Act (ADA), the law that's supposed to watch out for people like me, would surely come to the rescue, making it easier for me to get in and around places just like everyone else. Fat chance.

It soon became clear that ADA compliance is a box-checking exercise for builders and landlords alike. Much to everyone's surprise, ADA compliance doesn't actually mean that something is usable, as a practical matter, by someone who is disabled.

The list of places I could go unassisted was shrinking by the day. It's as though the designers of this world developed cities to make sure people who aren't ambulatory are unable to navigate the urban terrain, preferring us to stay locked away in our homes, out of sight. How many people do you see around your town with wheelchairs or walkers? Very few, I'm sure.

I was being kicked to the curb by society. I was silently being told, "Your kind doesn't belong here."

This book shines a spotlight on how our society treats those of us with disabilities by categorically ignoring, overlooking, and otherwise making us invisible. ALS was simply my VIP backstage pass into this experience.

As the disease progressed, I lost any real function of my hands, and speaking became a struggle to the point where I was frequently asked to repeat myself. Dressing, feeding myself, and any sort of self-care went out the window. I started writing this book using voice-to-text programs, but now I rely on eye-tracking technology to get my thoughts onto paper or to speak.

What does ALS feel like? Think about the coldest day you were outside. How did your arms and legs feel? Your fingers and toes? Stiff until they warmed up, right? With ALS, that stiffness never goes away—it never improves. Scratching your head was once so satisfying, and now you need someone's help. *If* you can get someone's attention, that is. And *if* the someone can understand what you're asking for.

It's not all doom and gloom, though. Parking is great, and I can behave like a cranky old man and say just about anything to anyone.

But the reality is that until there's a cure, I'm living in a long-term hospice.

2

What Makes Us Invisible?

THE PEOPLE ON THIS PLANET, like me, who don't look like everyone else—in an upright, bipedal, self-sufficient, and ambulatory kind of way—are invisible to their healthy peers or treated like second-class citizens.

This happens when we can't look a person in the eye while sitting in our wheelchair; when we can't navigate a dining room in a restaurant that claims it's accessible because the front door is wide enough; when people think we're stupid or drunk or, even worse, ignore us because they can't understand our unintelligible speech; when we're bumped into, knocked around, tripped over, and spilled on.

I'm not claiming that average ambulatory people go out of their way to ignore those of us afflicted with something that causes us to look physically different. What I am saying, based on my recent but limited experience, and after living in NYC for ten years, is that the world would rather not acknowledge the existence of those of us who are disabled.

The first notable time I was treated this way was at Newark Airport, on a trip home from Denver. A man and his son were walking through the baggage claim when I noticed the man had dropped his parking ticket. I tried to scream for him to pick up his ticket, but he and his son looked right past me as if I weren't there and kept walking.

When I finally rolled close enough to them, I said, "What I was trying to tell you was that you dropped your parking ticket. I have ALS and it affects my speech." What I also thought was, *This is a teachable moment for your son. Treat me like a human so he will too.*

A month or two later, my parents took me to an outstanding concert held in the back room of a beautiful piano shop in northern New Jersey. The majority of the audience was made up of people with ties to ALS. The pianist himself was going through the early stages of the disease. His unsteady movements and rapid exhaustion reminded me of my own situation when I was first diagnosed. He performed beautifully for just over an hour, but then he told the audience he didn't have the strength to continue. I understood completely.

Before we left, several people from the ALS community gathered around my parents and me to say hello. I spotted a few new faces. One woman in particular, who declared that her forty-seven-year-old son had ALS, turned to my mother and asked, "How old is he?"

Lady, I'm right here, alive and in front of you, I thought.

Smartly, my mother said, "Why don't you ask him?"

It's possible the woman assumed I wasn't verbal, like her son, or I was deaf. Or, more probable, she was being thoughtless. But she should have known better. I sure as hell shouldn't have to fight to be seen and heard within the disability community.

Mistake numero uno that people make when meeting me for the first time and seeing me in this chair is that I'm not intelligent or capable of communicating. It erodes my dignity when someone talks about me in front of me. And I feel infinitely worse when someone uses baby talk, like "there you go" or "c'mon, just one more itty-bitty bite."

And then there's the sidewalk.

When people walk down the sidewalk, or anywhere for that matter, they have an obligation as responsible human beings to watch where they're going. Important, though unspoken, rules govern good citizenship for pedestrians. You have every right to be outraged when those rules are flouted.

It happens all the time—someone will diddle with their phone for half a block and then look surprised and partly apologetic when they bump into me.

While I was using my crutches or walker, I was already unstable and couldn't dodge someone easily. A collision was certainly going to be worse for me than for the able-bodied guy. I've fallen countless times in public, and it's never graceful or pretty. But now that all 120 pounds of me are seated in a 450-pound motorized power chair, I've significantly changed the odds in my favor. Now when I'm not paying attention, sidewalk-rule-breakers might end up with a crushed toe if they bump into me.

In the same category, earning the first-place prize for offenders of the rules of the sidewalk, are those backward-baseball-hat-and ill-fitting-jean-wearing douchey ex-frat boys who walk together in a slop mob, shoulder to shoulder, spanning the width of the entire walkway. I appreciate the power walk in an attempt to exercise off what they're about to drink at a boozy brunch, but they take up the whole damn sidewalk.

Now that I'm driving a small Sherman tank, I have multiple targets to mess with, which means my ability to make this encounter awkward for all of them is greater than their ability to stop me. Maybe my hand will accidentally slip off the joystick of my power wheelchair, sending me careening into the middle of the douche gaggle.

It's not so much that I'm angry they're still able to enjoy their lives while mine has been turned upside down. It's more that I'm upset at their cluelessness.

I've also encountered my fair share of people going too far the other way. This is how it typically goes down.

I'm rolling along the sidewalk, no doubt being schlepped by one of my many friends kind enough to endure whatever activity I've convinced them is necessary to participate in, and someone, I'll call him Chad, comes walking along toward me. I know Chad wants to ascertain just what malady I've been plagued with. He can't help himself. So he stares.

When Chad realizes I've caught him staring, he looks me right in the eyes and smiles. It's as if he were saying to himself, *What the hell is wrong with him? Oh shit, he caught me. I'll flash a fake smile so he doesn't think I was gawking.*

How is it that I know Chad's thoughts so clearly?

Because I was guilty of them myself.

Though I'm relatively new to the disabled community, all it takes is one day to understand the extreme challenges—and to realize how unconscious you have been.

3

Staring at Asses and Crotches

"Do I give you the ass or the crotch?"
—Tyler Durden in *Fight Club*

WHEN I WAS SEVEN YEARS OLD, my parents took me to NYC and we rode the subway. At that tender age, I noticed that since I was so short, all I could see were people's butts. Now, thirty-two years later, I'm back in the same position—this time not due to my age or height.

It's not always bad, depending on who the butt belongs to.

Still, I've noticed things I'd really rather not, like the thin layer of filth covering all of NYC that I'm now destined to traipse through. Or how I'm now at eye level with the homeless, certain dogs, and the projectile flush spray from most toilets. Albeit far from the mind and view of my former able-bodied self, the world is disgusting at my new level, and there will never be enough hand sanitizer to wash that grime away.

In March 2018, I went to Irving, Texas, for a client meeting held in a facility the size of a Walmart with two additional floors. I could still walk with forearm crutches, but I knew I would surely tire out before I reached the conference room. What I needed was a motorized scooter. I had rented them before without much difficulty, though this would be the first time in a business setting.

So I called my usual scooter rental place and asked them to deliver the scooter to the hotel where I would be staying. Then I had to find an Uber with a big enough trunk for the scooter, as well as a driver willing and able to haul the thing in and out of the trunk.

When booking the Uber, I allowed sufficient time for any theatrics or mechanical difficulties, but that ended up not being necessary. The driver muscled the scooter into the trunk and off we went to the client site. While the meeting was important, I was more interested to see how a corporate office would accommodate the flame-red scooter and my novice driving skills.

As it turned out, the two days I was there weren't difficult physically, but I found being confined to the scooter frustrating from a business interaction perspective. Nearly thirty people were signed up for this meeting from across the United States, and when my team and I arrived in the lobby, it seemed as though everyone had arrived at once.

Negotiating the registration desk was the first test. I had to talk to the security guard whose eyes and ears were feet above mine. As if that weren't enough of a barrier, I had to reach above my head from a seated position to hand over my ID and contort awkwardly to be seen by the camera taking my badge picture.

Next came the elevator. The doors opened and the people inside weren't getting out. *Shit. Now what?*

"Watch your toes, I'm coming in," I said.

In hindsight, I should have backed in, making it easier to exit, but who doesn't enjoy breaking a few cultural norms? Try facing the wrong way next time you're in an elevator and watch the looks of discomfort on everyone's face.

Navigating the hallways and corridors of the sprawling carpeted ocean of cubicles proved to be fairly easy with the scooter. I arrived at the conference room and found that several of the attendees had already taken their seats. Normally this would be the time for me to make my way around to say hello to the people I knew, but traversing the chairs, briefcases, and shoulder bags strewn everywhere would make my greeting ritual impossible.

Thirty people were squeezed into a conference room designed to hold twelve. Although having the scooter meant I had my own seat and a nifty basket that held my belongings, the dimensions of the scooter made me overly obtrusive in the room. Self-conscious and distracted, I also realized I was locked into my parking space and would be unable to excuse myself easily. What if I had to use the bathroom? Forget about it.

The meeting itself went well, though I was distracted by the upcoming challenges awaiting me: Would it be hard to navigate back to the lobby elevator? Would the button be difficult to reach? Would there be closed doors and no one around to open them? How exactly would the bathroom work? Would I find the right type of Uber vehicle again? Heightened anxiety naturally comes along with this lovely diagnosis, and this experience made me realize why.

As the meeting wrapped up, everyone began to pair off, shake hands, and make plans to move their projects forward. Except me. I was trapped at a seated height while everyone talked above my head. I was sort of already used to this, being five foot seven and the shortest of my friends, but this was a humbling experience—being overlooked and excluded.

That experience spurred me on to find a way to get back in the game. I took an aggressive approach to this illness, buying things, often with the help of insurance, that I thought I would need before I had an emergency. The list included an extremely sophisticated wheelchair with the capability to raise the user to standing eye height.

This feature alone made a world of difference. I no longer missed out on being involved in a conversation. That was a great thing—both to help the conversation be more effective and to prevent the infuriating use of a subtle nonverbal technique that people employ when talking to someone in a regular-height wheelchair: My counterparts had to bend their necks down to look me in the eye. Once they were done talking, regardless of whether I was or not, they simply stood up straight and gazed over my head, ruling that the conversation was over, and there was nothing I could do to keep them engaged.

I was the unfortunate recipient of this technique more times than I care to count. While I prefer to give the other person the benefit of the doubt and chalk up their behavior to unintentional thoughtlessness, it did make me feel invalidated and invisible.

Never again. Now, with the seat elevator function on my new power wheelchair, I could look everyone in the eye.

4

Surprise, You're a Slob Now

I WAS ENDEARINGLY LABELED A metrosexual during my late twenties and into my thirties. Living in NYC in the prime of my life, I dressed like I had stepped out of *GQ* magazine. Well-tailored suit, neatly folded pocket square in my breast pocket, designer socks, and polished shoes. It was entirely possible that I looked like a total ass, but I owned the look, the walk, and the attitude, and I carried a line of bullshit that made dating enjoyable.

I joined a competitive sailing team out of Oyster Bay, New York, a program that eventually grew into Oakcliff Sailing, a training center led by Dawn Riley, captain of the America's Cup and the Ocean Race. Add a budding running career to my social résumé, and I had plenty to brag about.

Of course, all of that came to a grinding halt.

With ALS, the muscles throughout your entire body stiffen up, making a full range of motion impossible, or at the very least extremely difficult. Robbed of my fine motor skills first, I had to cut out many of the fun activities and look for shortcuts to simplify my daily routine: *Maybe I don't need to shave today. I brushed my teeth this morning, so why do I need to do it again?*

Those shortcuts can turn into habits, and before you know it, you haven't taken a shower in three days, you're wearing a Snuggie, and you might even have a pee bag strapped to your leg.

I struggled with both dexterity and reach. When it came to grooming, I figured out that I could reach the top of my head to comb my hair by sitting on the toilet and leaning on the sink. This accounted for the front and top, but what about the back? If I was going to wear a mullet, I might as well wear it proudly.

Shaving anything became dangerous. The angles and techniques critical to ensuring I didn't commit suicide each morning were a real concern for me as they are for every man of beard-growing age. Over time, my fingers cramped into the closed-fisted clawlike shape they remain in now, and my electric razor would no longer fit in my hand.

On the positive side, hipster scruff was stylish, and I could get away with a three- or four-day growth and still look reasonably presentable. But post-shave, opening that small, expensive tube of skin cream was a nonstarter. And nothing tweezable was tweezed. Brushing my teeth became more difficult, though the electric toothbrush was a godsend—until I couldn't hold it anymore.

Although NYC breeds a particular uniform consisting of as much black as possible, I had always needed to differentiate myself. I had amassed quite a wardrobe, ranging from sharp custom business attire to casual weekend gear that was always a step above the norm.

Now when it was time to get dressed, my focus changed from what looked best for the occasion to what was easiest to get onto my body. Button-down shirts were difficult, not only to get on over my shoulders because of my limited range of motion but also to actually button. Being the clever and innovative man that I am, I used a combination of a long shoehorn, the back of a chair, and a brilliant device called a button hooker to get my dress shirts on. What a sight!

Pants were slightly easier until I began losing grip strength, which also made putting on socks all the more difficult. Most people don't give socks a second thought, but when you have ALS, you become aware of how snug your socks are, how high they come up your leg, and how quickly you want to rocket them out the window when the heel doesn't sit right where it's supposed to. Sockless became my new fashion statement for as long as my ankles could tolerate the cold.

Tying laces became far too cumbersome for me, eventually necessitating alternative footwear. Mind you, I'll never ever, even under pain of swollen feet, ganglion cysts, and longer-than-appropriate toenails, purchase or wear Crocs. I'll leave those to Mario Batali and six-year-olds.

Okay, all ready to walk out of the door? You're still ambulatory, so sure. Well, not so fast. First, you need to plan every step you're about to take. And where will you put your keys so you can easily get them out when you come home? Is that jacket pocket where you put your cell phone too tight for you to dig out your phone when it rings? If you *can* reach your phone, which earphones will you use to answer the call? Screw the phone, that's why there's voicemail.

Don't forget your wallet. Where are you going to place it so your barely usable hands can access it later? How will you get your wallet out of your pants? This one is fun when you need to ask your friends, or better yet, a stranger, for help.

Thirty minutes later, you're finally ready to leave the house. Since driving is out of the question, what are your options? Phoning a friend works once, maybe twice. The New Jersey Transit system has short buses for its Access Link, but the local county-run Access Link or Access-a-Ride doesn't leave the county, so it's on you, my poor invalid friend, to coordinate the transfer.

Far be it from them to give a shit when they dump you in a supermarket parking lot to wait for the next county's van to show up. And I hope that you're not obviously disabled, because you'll likely be passed by in favor of a more able-bodied passenger.

Uber is no better, given its track record of discrimination against disabled passengers.

Hailing a cab? Good luck maneuvering to the curb and raising your arm. But even if you do manage to get a cab to stop, you have to grapple with all sorts of questions: What type of vehicle is it? An SUV? There's no chance you're getting into it on your own. Which side of the taxi do you get into? Do you get out on the same side or somehow switch sides independently? With sedans and vehicles lower to the ground, how will you stand up on your own?

Not all cabbies are alike, and you might stumble upon a thoughtful one. Through the goodness of their hearts, some of them will do anything possible to help you into and out of their cab.

All this planning and awkward shuffling took a toll on my energy level and ate up the precious hours in a day. (And this doesn't even include medical appointments.) What gave way was self-care. As much as I tried to stay neatly groomed and looking sharp, I was finding less and less time each day to pay attention to things that weren't absolutely critical. As my appearance took a hit, my self-confidence began to circle the drain.

The feeling of helplessness was overwhelming. My daily routine needed careful choreography for even the most basic tasks. But the planning couldn't start too far in advance since overthinking the day might kick off a bout of anxiety. And the planning couldn't start too late because that would cause me to rush, get hurt, and then ultimately be late anyway. I continually found myself operating in a world that couldn't and wouldn't accommodate my needs.

What no one tells you about the journey into becoming disabled are all the small things you must figure out for yourself. Sure, there are books and blogs and social workers to guide you, but your journey is an individual one, and it's a clusterfuck of unwanted surprises.

How could I have known that a T-shirt getting stuck as I pulled it over my head would set off a panic attack? Or that an itch I couldn't scratch on my own would cause spikes of rage sharp enough to start a small world war? Or worst of all, that I would feel such unimaginable grief when I could no longer hug a loved one?

It's been painful watching my friends and family try to figure out the right way to approach me, the right things to say. How not to hurt me. I've said to them, "Just hug me, touch me, I won't break. I need physical contact more than ever. And please don't stop spending time with me because you're afraid of doing the wrong thing. The worst thing is to avoid me."

The list of things that now take inordinate amounts of time is long. Right up there with self-care and basic functioning is communication. ALS patients are often referred to as being "locked in" because the disease robs them of the ability to communicate. The technology that helps me overcome many of the communication challenges, such as the Tobii Dynavox PCEye Mini eye tracker that I used to write this book, is nothing short of miraculous.

Nonetheless, 20 words per minute is as fast as this technology will allow me to "type" with my eyes. Considering the average person can type around 50 words per minute and can speak at a rate of over 120 words per minute, I'm seriously struggling to keep up with written and spoken forms of communication. Honestly, though, no matter how good the technology is, the pace at which my symptoms evolve makes each bit of technology obsolete almost as fast as I can master it.

In the early stages of the disease, as everything that had made me the man I was—my independence and strength—started to wither away, I was finding excuses not to leave the house and not to break from the routine that gave me what little comfort and normalcy was possible.

My walking speed slowed, my balance faltered, and crossing the street unassisted became impossible. I frequently questioned my own ability to make it through the day. Was I stable enough today? Was the wind going to knock me off balance? Were the sidewalks busy, and would I get bumped into? Would someone open—and hold—the door for me? What if there were no handrail?

To add insult to injury, when I had no obvious signs of a disability and asked for help, I was often scowled at or blatantly ignored.

One of the last business meetings I attended in person was at the office of my number one client in Jersey City, New Jersey. The office building is beautifully situated on the western bank of the Hudson River, but it's crazy windy, and even the most sure-footed person has trouble walking. I struggled my way out of the Uber and began to traverse the hundred or so feet toward the large glass double doors into the lobby, where my colleagues were waiting for me.

The wind was howling, and the shape of the building's entrance only magnified the frequent gusts. Laptop bag on my shoulder, I was being spun around every which way. I needed something to grab hold of to steady myself. The railing at the ice-skating rink of my youth sprang to mind.

Flattening myself against the wall of the building, I decided to wait for the next lull in the wind, then inch toward the doors. I pressed my hands flat against the bricks behind me, grasping the texture, looking for any place to grip that would steady me. I contemplated calling one of my colleagues to come peel me off the wall and drag me to the safety of the lobby, but my phone was unreachable. I could just see my watch poking out of my sleeve, alerting me to the fact that I was about to make the team late.

Pinned there for what felt like an eternity, cautiously inching my way toward the doors, I was making poor progress. One or two of the passers-by noticed I was standing there, but to them it must have looked like I was one of the smokers who usually huddled in that filthy corner of the entrance where the leaves and garbage swirled around. Finally, I managed to shuffle close enough to the door, and someone offered to open it for me.

Only the two coworkers I was meeting knew about my ALS. I had kept it under pretty tight wraps from the company I worked for and from my clients, not because I was afraid of anyone knowing what I was going through, but because I wanted to focus on my job and not let the disease become a distraction.

That day dealt a crushing blow to my spirit and ego and any sense that I was going to overcome this easily.

5

Eating Ain't What It Used to Be

FOOD IS AN IMPORTANT PART of my life. I refuse to use the nouveau-hipster word "foodie" to identify myself because, frankly, it has no actual meaning anymore. It's been diluted by every Instagram and Twitter influencer wannabe to the point where the word means nothing more than someone who is discerning of the food they eat.

What's important is my personal food experience, such as the smell and flavor you get from an overstuffed, medium-rare mushroom Swiss burger with brioche bun—pure ecstasy. Wash it down with an extra-dirty, chilled Hendrick's martini, and it won't matter if the world collapses around you.

As the strength and dexterity in my hands continued to diminish, picking up the burger, the martini, or even utensils in general became too difficult. Soup was a catastrophe. Food dropped out of my hands onto my lap, and my face was covered in dried bits of whatever I had eaten. I was embarrassed. More than that, I was ashamed—not of ALS, but of the mess I had become. And I was mourning the slow loss of the dignified and proud man I had been.

Eventually, I stopped being so concerned with the quality and types of food I was eating and focused on finding things that were easier to open and consume. The less preparation required, the better. But even that little bit of independence began to slip as the weakness started to make its way up my arms. That juicy hamburger now needed to be cut into pieces for me so I could eat it with a spoon. This, as anyone in the burger-loving world knows, is a sacrilegious way to eat one of nature's most perfect foods.

Drinks also became tough to manage. When you ask waiters for a straw to accompany your martini, watch the panic flash across their faces as they try to evaluate how rapidly the night will turn into a shit show as you guzzle what's essentially a full glass of gin like a frat guy showing off.

One of my favorite restaurants is Avenue in Long Branch, New Jersey. Not because the food is particularly exceptional, but because it's right on the beach, it's wheelchair accessible, the stylish dining room has soaring ceilings and stunning decor, and the well-curated Eastern European waiting staff are modelesque (and out of my league).

When I could still eat somewhat normally, I went there for lunch and ordered a medium rare gourmet burger and their signature gin gimlet. I told the waitress, "Please cut the burger in half and serve the gimlet in a rocks glass rather than a martini glass."

She scurried off and came back with a concerned look on her face. "Sir, I'm sorry, but the bartender said he won't put that drink in a rocks glass."

What an asshole. "I totally know this isn't your fault," I said. "If you wouldn't mind, please impress upon the bartender that your customer is in a wheelchair and can't hold a martini glass. If you feel you can't make that clear, then I will, and it will involve the manager and the town, and it will be a very different kind of conversation."

My drink arrived in a rocks glass a few minutes later.

Once a source of great pleasure, food has become a frustrating daily annoyance. I no longer look forward to eating since every food type comes with its own set of challenges. Being fed by someone else is not only a degrading and infantilizing experience—it's also messy. If you're headed to where I am, you might need to instruct your caregivers on three primary rules.

Basic aiming. This shouldn't require a dissertation in applied geometry, but the basics seem lost on many folks. Think about the game where you feed a baby and you pretend the spoon is an airplane delivering a precious cargo of food. Approach the runway, line up centered with the mouth, level out, and insert spoon into the mouth. Watch out for the teeth on your way into the hangar, and don't, by any measure, graze the cheeks, plastering food cargo outside the drop zone.

Here's a biggie. During this process, food inevitably gets everywhere. Every caregiver should—for the love of God—please refrain from picking droppings off the person/the table/the napkin and inserting them back into the person's mouth with anything other than the appropriate utensil. I don't know about you, but jamming multiple fingers into my mouth only makes this already degrading experience that much worse. (Besides, caregiver, you've been pushing me around all day, and I know you haven't washed your hands.)

Cleanup is part of the job. By the time I'm done, I look like a product of those fed-up parents on a plane who gave up caring somewhere over Racine, Wisconsin, and let their terrorist children destroy a galley kitchen full of snacks, leaving the cleanup job for someone else. The caregiver, on the other hand, does not get to ignore the mess. No way is it okay to leave me and my pride covered in a mess.

Pills, like food, are a daily requirement. Taking pills was simple enough at the beginning. I would open a cell in my handy pill organizer (meticulously set up to sort and place those tiny pills), dump everything into my hand, and gobble them down like a reverse Pez dispenser. Over time, the number of pills increased, and the shapes and sizes changed so much that my apartment began to look like a Vitamin Shoppe store. When I came across an article touting the benefits of some new plant or bizarre vitamin, I ordered it and added it to the daily regimen.

The color of my urine began to change with whatever new supplements I took, which isn't a big deal typically, since I'm fairly used to lighter or darker shades of yellow. But when you look down and green comes out, you tend to panic, as I did. Had I caught something during that one-night stand with the creature from *The Shape of Water*? But it didn't matter what effect the supplements had—I was determined to try everything all at once.

Eventually, the pills didn't go down as easily anymore, and it was taking longer to finish them. My father came up with a brilliant idea of purchasing "00" capsules online and jamming as many pills as possible into a single capsule. This drastically reduced the quantity I had to take each day, but even this became difficult, necessitating that we crush everything with a mortar and pestle and mix it into applesauce.

ALS presents its own unique challenges to eating, and it's not just the food-handling issue. Once a properly sized morsel of food was placed into my mouth, I began the challenge of chewing and swallowing. My tongue was losing strength and control, my cheeks got in the way, and I salivated uncontrollably.

When I managed to chew the bit of food sufficiently and decided to swallow, it was a crapshoot whether it would go down or get stuck on the roof of my mouth or on the very back of my tongue. Regardless of the location, food getting stuck caused a panic response, and I ended up gagging violently. This triggered my eyes to water, my limbs and torso to cramp, my nose to run, and excess saliva to come out. Not to mention some unpleasant noises, which I had no control over. This happened with every meal.

Those unfortunate folks outside my immediate family who got to witness this spectacle? I watched them through my watering eyes as they averted their gaze, hoping the scene I was making quickly came to an end. I know they felt helpless and wished they could help, but everyone had to be patient because most of the time I simply needed to ride it out.

What did help was covering my mouth, not in a smothering-me-with-a-pillow kind of way, but just enough to prevent any projectiles from crossing the room. It was more of a dignity play than anything else. Plus, it ensured everyone's face and clothes stayed food-free.

This chain reaction caused me to be selective about where and when I ate. Being at home was safe, but being out in public or with my family and friends was highly concerning. I frequently found myself declining most of the meal in fear that I'd disrupt the occasion. When my throat began to tighten or my tongue got tired, it was time to sit back and take a break from eating—or it would turn into "The Jeremy Show."

Despite my reservations about eating out, on Mother's Day in 2019, we took my mother to Catch 19 in Red Bank, New Jersey, as part of a weekend of pampering, appreciation, and great eating. This restaurant is quite the Jersey scene, with highly styled decor, incredible food, and overly loud music. It's the kind of place I would have dragged my buddies to when things were good.

While the volume of music coming from the live band six feet away from our table made it impossible to hear one another, my mother pointed out that it would also drown out my gagging and choking noises. She was right about the slop show I was about to star in. We made a good decision to face me toward the wall.

It was time for a feeding tube.

Many of the PALS (People with ALS) I've spoken with agree that the feeding tube significantly improved their quality of life, effectively ending the struggle to eat and take medicines. While they can still eat normally, the tube gives them an easier option when they're tired or sick. Clearly my self-image is important to me, and I was quite satisfied with the one frontal protrusion I already had.

But having lost over thirty pounds since this all started, I was by now a sickly one hundred pounds. I needed the tube.

I had toughed it out long enough, thinking I could eat enough calories by mouth to keep me full and maintain the much-needed weight. But I was choking more often, the excess saliva was uncontrollable, and I was hungry a lot of the time. There's no award for struggling the most while eating, so I needed to make this tube happen as soon as possible—especially since medical journals say that mortality rates are more than three times higher for underweight patients.

I was walking on thin ice.

After reaching out to several gastrointestinal doctors, I found that I couldn't get a simple consultation inside of a month. Who knew July was the high season for feeding tube installations? I began to panic. The mortality rate and statistics being what they were, I calculated I wouldn't survive past the end of the year.

A diagnosis with a short expiration date forces you to face your own mortality on an almost daily basis. Every decision becomes about either making yourself more comfortable or getting your affairs in order so your loved ones aren't saddled with the burden of whatever you leave behind. Refusing to become a statistic, I wanted a fighting chance.

Having friends in medicine can be useful in situations like this. But they're all in the wrong specialties: podiatry, anesthesia, dermatology. I even have a friend who works in a fancy vagina spa. That concept blows my mind. As a fan of vaginas, I can't help but wonder what services are offered. And can you send gift certificates? With what message? Despite my ruminations on behalf of the entire vagina-owning community, clearly that expertise wasn't going to serve me now.

My close friend Randee has worked in the operating room for almost fifteen years, so I hoped she would offer an easy solution. I texted her, asking what I should do to accelerate this process, especially if I took a turn for the worse. Without hesitating, she insisted I go to the emergency room. But no way was I handing my already slim chance of survival to some bleary-eyed medical school resident at the end of a thirty-six-hour shift.

After some creative maneuvering around the local physician pool and learning a few key phrases that made gatekeeping office managers snap to attention, such as "failure to thrive," I had myself an appointment two days later in one of the area's premier gastrointestinal medical practices. The following week, I was wheeled into an operating room at Morristown Medical Center. One hour later, I woke up with a second body part I could use to do the helicopter. (Men, you know what I'm talking about. If you've forgotten, ask your son.)

I can easily say this was a good decision. The weight I've gained is helping me sleep better, I'm more comfortable since I'm not all boney, I'm less depressed, and I'm regaining strength.

It's not all fun and games, though. While nothing prevents me from "eating for pleasure," as it's called, I must get the majority of my calories through the tube, which is quite a rigmarole.

The culinary journey began with four "feedings" spread throughout the day. Each feeding consisted of a 250 milliliter container of a beige slurry of essential nutrients and amino acids made by our friends at the Nestlé company. Mornings and nights, the regimen of medications were pulverized, diluted, and funneled into my gut. I didn't miss the pill process. And once we began adding five milligrams of liquid cannabis to my formula each morning, mealtime became a lot more fun.

That ended abruptly when I started getting nauseated immediately after each feeding. There are several theories on what causes this, though at first glance, it seemed obvious: the formula was all chemicals. That, and I may have been fed too quickly. It's as if the entire meal, including the drink, suddenly lands in your stomach.

After trying two different formulas, also from Nestlé, and failing to eliminate nausea and diarrhea, we took the advice of some others with tube feeding experience and began blending my food. Although this allowed us to control everything I ate, it was a complete disaster, not to mention a huge waste of food with all the experimentation.

It isn't as simple as making your usual dinner and then scraping your plate into the blender. No amount of high-powered blending in a turbocharged Vitamix will help get that steak through my feeding tube, let alone out the other end.

You must consider each attribute of the food, such as solubility in water, viscosity, calorie density, nutritional value, and propensity to bind or loosen. Of course, regular allergen considerations don't go away, so you have to pay attention to allergies and sensitivities too. The best part is that if your caregivers can't cook for shit and habitually burn water, it won't matter, since you won't taste it!

Blending my food proved unsustainable, not only because it took so much effort to produce each meal, but also because the ingredients and equipment didn't travel well. So after all the trial and error with my poor tummy, we finally landed on a feeding-tube-friendly formulation that wasn't chock-full of chemicals. I'd get real food. Real, actual food. In fact, it's called Real Food Blends. It comes in a hermetically sealed bag and is covered by insurance.

Thankfully, one aspect of my hygiene regimen doesn't require human intervention—going to the bathroom. Nothing is more comforting than the familiarity of your own toilet in your own house. The height, the shape, the privacy, and, most importantly, the predictable quality of the toilet paper. Is there anything worse than encountering the single-ply shiny and nonabsorptive quality of Scott's found at most workplaces? You may as well use a page from the *New York Post*.

I know what you're thinking—if his hands don't work, how does he wipe his ass? Great question. This was one of my biggest concerns as my dexterity diminished. There's a brilliant invention that European asses have been enjoying for centuries: the bidet. It's simple, hygienic, and environmentally friendly, and it gives your morning constitutional a "how do you do!"

Five months after my diagnosis, when I moved back into my parents' house to get better care, I ordered bidets for every toilet. The controls were on a panel firmly mounted at the back-right side, requiring a contorted twist of my torso to reach. What I didn't account for was the stiffening of my shoulders and arms, making it more and more difficult to reach the controls. But, hell, I'm determined to struggle because the result is refreshingly satisfying.

I had some upcoming travel, so my concerns about the "toileting process," as it's called in the healthcare world, weren't completely solved. As a grown man, I wanted nothing to do with someone else wiping my ass. I considered a few options to avoid this degrading scenario. I could save it until I was home from the trip, eat only things that were constipating, such as steak and hard cheeses, or I could meditate away the need to go.

None of these options being ideal, I found an exciting alternative to a probable trip to the hospital. The Japanese toilet manufacturer Toto has created a handheld, battery-operated, portable, and oh-so-delightful little bidet that works wonders when traveling. Nobel Prize material, definitely.

6

Parking Assholes

THE ADA REQUIRES ALL PUBLIC buildings to have a sufficient number of accessible parking spaces. Generally speaking, the ADA calls for one accessible spot for every twenty-five total spots. But it sure feels like it's more about *in*sufficiency, as though they determine the number of people entitled to use the accessible parking and then reduce the number of corresponding spaces by the average number of rainy days in that zip code. As a result, at least 35 percent of disabled visitors are forced to park somewhere far less accessible.

Just about anyone with a doctor's note can obtain a disability placard. Some have googled themselves into having fibromyalgia, others have support peacocks that can't walk long distances, and still others feel generally entitled. They can all ask their doctors to write a prescription to get a premium parking spot complete with bragging rights. Congratulations to them on successfully scamming the system.

No disability placard or license plate? Then that person better stay the hell out of my spot. And for that matter, they better stay out of my bathroom stall too. (Their feet probably don't reach the floor anyway.)

What probably isn't obvious to average people is the exhausting amount of preparation and labor that led up to our being able to leave the house and arrive at the parking spot they've been eyeing. Those of us in legitimate need of this privileged spot suffer enough as it is.

Of course, if violators need a gentle reminder of why they shouldn't park in my precious spot, the local meter maid will gladly issue them a ticket. If they've hit the jackpot, they may even get to visit their car in the local impound lot. Helping a meter maid find parking offenders is my contribution to making parking great again.

I understand feeling lazy, wanting to park as close as possible because it's raining, or planning to be "just be a minute," but I can promise that you will think twice about parking in my much-needed space after liberating your car from impoundment. There's a special place in hell for lazy asses, right alongside Hitler, robocallers, and whoever invented that impossible-to-open plastic packaging.

I've often considered creating a bumper sticker that offending parkers can have as a badge of honor—something to help other drivers understand the type of person they really are. Something along the lines of "I abuse the crippled." Yes, using those words exactly. The sticker would be printed on that impossible-to-remove, easily frayed material. As an alternative, my sadistic and very close friends Laura Hickey and Pat McCartney suggested keeping it simple and keying a deep groove on the side of the offender's car.

For legitimate disabled drivers, lessons are here for you too. As much as you hate the able-bodied people illegally taking our spots, it doesn't entitle you to park badly. Simply park between the two blue lines—otherwise, I have to figure out how to maneuver around your land yacht with enough space to extend my van's ramp and roll myself into the lot without scraping the paint off your doors. It's difficult enough being us, living this life filled with pain and suffering, so let's make a pact to be kind to one another, shall we?

With all the accessible transit options out there, my least favorite is the short bus. These stripped-down, rusted-out, and repurposed bread trucks of yesteryear are a sad excuse for safe, reliable, and dignified transportation. No one involved enjoys the experience, van drivers included. Their job sucks, I get it. They get twelve dollars an hour to haul my unhelpful body to and from my various appointments, hoping for some semblance of normal conversation, which will never come. It's a lonely existence for both of us.

But I'm a human being and expect to be treated with dignity. Drivers beware that if I receive something short of civil treatment, I'll be sure to use my endless amount of free time figuring out ways to make their jobs worse. Did I forget to fully close my pee bag before I got into the van? Maybe I messed up the appointment dates and have to go back home, but not before being unloaded once or twice.

As a driver responsible for the well-being of the disabled and elderly, a short bus driver should be conscientious about where and how he parks his massive van. An argument that he'll only be in front of the entrance for a minute is a gross misjudgment of time (namely mine) and space (namely his).

Vans for individuals with disabilities in other countries also leave much to be desired. The idea of passenger safety isn't high on anyone's list of priorities to be solved. Broken shocks, flimsy tie-down straps, doors secured with an old leather belt, and entrance ramps at unusually steep angles all make for an ass-puckering, real-life roller coaster.

When I used to ride the bus in NYC, someone in a wheelchair would occasionally want to board. It amazed me that the city had accommodation for disabled passengers on public transit. (I would later come to learn how limited this service really is.) The process of getting that person on and off the bus was nothing short of impressive.

The driver had to get out, lower the bus, flip out the ramp, get the person into the bus, tell people to move from the seats reserved for people with disabilities, flip up those seats, and then go through the painful process of securing the wheelchair to the bus. A well-trained bus driver and an accommodating herd of passengers could whip through this process before the next traffic light change.

While my fellow able-bodied passengers and I watched this operation with wonderment, the underlying annoyance of this time-sucking inconvenience was written on our faces. The name for that annoyance is selfishness—I'm complaining about being late while this guy is stuck in a wheelchair. Looks like I learned a hard lesson.

7

Accessible Isn't

"The person who designs a house
should be forced to live in it."
—Fred Schreiber

SOME PRODUCTS ARE BUILT WITH intentional design omissions, such as the Microsoft Surface tablet, which had only one USB slot. Useless. Others are designed in a vacuum with no input from the user community, such as my personal cannabis vaporizer pen, the PAX 3. It's beautiful to look at, but manipulating it with my hand is another story. It's also useless.

For sure, the designers of the things we use and the places we visit don't give enough careful consideration to usability by a wide range of people. The minor details an able-bodied person encounters each day can be insurmountable obstacles for a disabled person. A heavy door, steps, a curb without a good ramp, lack of a handrail, cluttered aisles and walkways, hard-to-open packaging.

I can't use much of the design I've encountered recently, and, I would imagine, neither can the majority of disabled people. What would be the incentive to thoughtfully design products and environments to allow everyone to use them? The answer is nothing. Zero. Zip. Zilch. Nada. There's no positive return on investing in another grab bar or a push-button door opener. Forget about the disabled. How many could there possibly be anyway?

Turns out there are enough of us to make ourselves heard. According to the US Centers for Disease Control and Prevention, 26 percent of adults (one in four) in the United States are disabled—that's roughly sixty-one million of us.

We do have some power as a group. In 2008, the ADA was updated and made more inclusive by broadening the definition of "disability." The federal law prohibits discrimination against people with disabilities in areas of public life, including access to public places and to private places open to the public. It also establishes standards for accessible design, like creating automatic doorways, ramps, and elevators to accommodate wheelchairs. (You can find helpful information on the ADA National Network website, and a complete set of laws and regulations on the ADA.gov website.)

But three caveats. First, while the rules are extensive, I have come to learn they aren't widely adhered to or enforced. I could point fingers (and I do), but bottom line, things don't get fixed unless enough people care that they're broken, so it's up to us in the disabled community to make some noise about compliance. We have to be strong advocates for legal progress—from small efforts to monumental ones, from grassroots campaigns to national crusades.

Second, even if the ADA were perfectly implemented, it only gets us so far because its mandates apply to limited public places and certain private places.

Third—and this is critical—there's a huge difference between being ADA compliant and being usable in a practical way that doesn't restrict access and availability.

Compliant is a grab bar in proximity to the toilet. Unusable is the toilet paper out of reach. Compliant is a thirty-six-inch door opening. Unusable is a door without an automatic opener. Compliant is a curb cut to allow an easy transition from the street to the sidewalk. Unusable is a broken sidewalk on the other side of the curb cut.

Builders, architects, and engineers should include a person with a disability to test drive the design before the first shovel of dirt is removed.

When it comes to horrible design, the worst example is the house I grew up in and where my parents and I live today. The split-level home is a strong front-runner for the Shortsighted Design of the Year Award. Rooms are grouped three per level, a staircase of six stairs joining each one. In my house, six separate levels make up a four-bedroom home. And that doesn't include the six steps from the walkway to the front door.

This means that if you're reading the paper in the living room and need to take a piss, you have your choice of going upstairs or downstairs. Not a big deal for that one task, but when you consider your entire day and how many times you move from room to room, it's a lot of ups and downs. Definitely not a usable design if you have weak knees or shortness of breath, if you're elderly or disabled, or God forbid, if you find yourself all the way in the den when you're high with a case of the munchies.

When I had to move out of my apartment and back home, my parents and I panicked, trying to figure out how to accommodate my changing needs. Which floor was best for me to live on? What modifications should be made first? Forget all that, how the hell do I even get into the house? Many difficult decisions had to be made quickly.

Stair glides were the first order of business. Typically made for hauling Grandma up the stairs, they became lifesavers until a more permanent solution could be devised. We needed to have a serious family conversation to decide whether to move into a newer and more accessible house or modify the house we were in. Either option was going to have a major impact on our lives.

Ultimately, we decided to stay put and modify the house. Little did we know what an undertaking this would be. Fortunately, through the efforts of a GoFundMe campaign, I reconnected with an old friend from college who happened to work for Steve Cohen of Steven S. Cohen Architects, a firm based in Princeton, New Jersey, that specializes in designing accessible buildings. Steve and his team partnered with a local builder to create a masterpiece of functionality and design that would accommodate my needs.

Everything had to be on one level. As my condition progressed, the stair glides that helped me traverse the multitude of levels to get to my bedroom became difficult to use. As simple as the glides are, my body protested the contortions I had to make to fit into the standard shape of the chair.

Next, I had to rethink everything I did throughout the day that would become increasingly difficult as my symptoms worsened—like the bathtub with the sliding glass door and nowhere to grab when I needed to steady myself, the bidet with out-of-reach controls, and a sink I couldn't get near. That was just one room.

Critically important, transferring me from one place to another had become a terrifying and risky experience for everyone involved, and that added stress was definitely not welcome.

I had to channel my inner Nostradamus to figure out what I would need to allow me to age in place. Top on the list: a roll-in shower, smooth transitions between rooms, a ceiling lift to take me from the bed to the toilet to the shower, a platform lift to get me from the living area to the exercise room or outside, and a washer and dryer that weren't in the basement.

I hope that I designed the space thoughtfully enough that my parents will use it once I no longer need it, allowing them to age in place the way they deserve.

A word of caution: The builder told us the project would take about four months, but it actually dragged on for a year and a half. After using the new space for a few weeks, we discovered the poor quality of his workmanship. If you modify your house as we did, inspect everything before making your final payment. Or hire a project manager to help. Family caregivers, like my parents, are often too busy helping their loved one to take on the task. The extra expense is well worth it.

After moving to my parents' home in New Jersey, I needed to find new care providers in the area. We were told that Kessler's outpatient program was the best for neurology-focused rehabilitation. After all, it's where Christopher Reeve went after his accident. If it's good enough for Superman, it's good enough for me.

What I had at Kessler was an altogether different and, frankly, disappointing experience. The bathrooms in the main lobby of the outpatient center were not only disgusting but also nowhere close to being either ADA compliant or accessible: they lacked push-button door openers, sufficient grab bars, toilet paper dispensers within reach, and a sink I could roll up to.

Add to that a senior office administrator who explained she was much too busy to answer the phone and return calls and didn't even acknowledge me when I rolled right in front of her in my wheelchair. The condition of this facility was unacceptable, and for my own health and safety, something needed to be done to address these deficiencies.

In addition to the poor quality of the facility itself, I faced tremendous difficulty with the various lines of service, such as physical and occupational therapy, the wheelchair clinic, and administration. By the way patients flowed through the outpatient rehabilitation center, I suspected that Kessler's priority was collecting my insurance rather than providing good patient care.

So in December 2018, I employed my own top-down method to escalate these issues to someone high up in the Kessler organization who would have the authority and incentive to finally solve the problems. Fifteen minutes after reaching someone in the administration, I received a call from the CEO of Kessler's local campus.

By the way, she isn't disabled, nor is anyone on her staff. Not that having a disability is a prerequisite for working in a hospital's administration, but it would lend some helpful perspective.

I was impressed with how understanding she was and how quickly she looked into resolving my concerns. She went so far as to send me a letter that expressed her commitment to addressing the issues and elaborated on how important patient satisfaction was to her personally and to Kessler as a whole. She also introduced me to her market director of plant operations and physical and occupational therapy leaders.

Months later, having received no further communications from the CEO or anyone on her staff, I visited the facility to see what modifications had actually been made. The only improvement was a fresh coat of paint in one bathroom. (Surely that tiny change to aesthetics would be easily justifiable in court when the judge asked the CEO what had been done to ensure ADA compliance.)

Disappointed, I went home and followed up with the CEO. I received this stunning email reply: "Our decision at this time is not to make any changes to the current setup. While you are visiting our facility, should you need assistance, our staff would be happy to help."

Really? Which staff member, exactly, would be assigned to assist me in the bathroom? How would I get their help and how quickly could they come running?

Reading between the lines, I got their message loud and clear: I didn't matter. My dignity was pushed aside with a dismissive email. *Maybe I'll roll over to their office after I finish a pot of coffee and a shrimp and mayo sandwich that has spent too much time out of the refrigerator.* Speaking of dropping bombs, my father has a great T-shirt that shows a B-52 airplane dropping bombs, with the caption "When diplomacy fails . . ."

This wasn't over. It was time to ask New Jersey Governor Phil Murphy for help. The *Star-Ledger* newspaper would enjoy a story about a nationally recognized healthcare institute discriminating against the very people it commits to serve. (*Publisher's note*: Jeremy never had a chance to follow up.)

In his February 8, 2019, article, "Where Luxury Meets Accessibility," *New York Times* author C. J. Hughes wrote about the scale of discrimination that occurs in the real estate market in NYC. This issue is actually pervasive across the largest real estate development companies, such as Related Companies, the Durst Organization, and Equity Residential, each named in the article.

New apartment buildings are being built at a record pace, but little is being done to include important accessibility accommodations. In his article, Hughes quotes Fred Freiberg, the executive director of the Fair Housing Justice Center, a nonprofit that hires testers to investigate buildings: "Compliance is more the exception than the rule. We still have a long way to go."

This is systematic discrimination against a large segment of the population. Prompted by the overwhelming number of complaints lodged with the Justice Department's Disability Rights section, CBS News correspondent Steve Dorsey reported on the subject in an article dated June 28, 2019: "Bad Braille Plagues Buildings across US, CBS News Radio Investigation Finds." Once it reaches this level of visibility, we can no longer assume that avoidance of compliance is unintentional.

As disability rights attorney and author Lainey Feingold said, "Sadly, compliance with federal and state laws and regulations often doesn't happen. There isn't the attention to detail around accessibility as there is to other issues like security and privacy when really it is all the same."

My experience tells me that many businesses are still operating under the defunct grandfather clause. That isn't a big surprise.

Without strict oversight, why would they cough up the money for changes?

When I followed a brief regimen of stem cell treatments (which didn't help me), I went to a clinic in New York housed in a building clearly not up to the 1991 ADA standards. Among other things, the office lacked an accessible bathroom—I couldn't sit down without hitting my knees on the sink in front of me, let alone maneuver a wheelchair.

Considering the way shady stem cell clinics in the United States have been investigated for claiming to cure every ailment imaginable, I suspect the doctor took my money and every other patient's and bought himself a Ferrari.

8

Wheels in the Sky

IF FOR SOME REASON YOU forget you're disabled, book yourself a flight and you'll be quickly reminded. Most airports have figured out disability access really well, but the airlines appear to have written the non-able-bodied out of the design of their aircraft.

My parents and I decided to take one of those once-in-a-lifetime trips to visit friends and family in Israel. We did tons of prep work to ensure every part would be accessible—the hotel rooms, the tours, especially the airplanes themselves.

After the United States passed the ADA in 1990, many other countries followed by enacting similar acts and laws. In 1998, the Israeli Knesset passed the Equal Rights for Persons with Disabilities law. Only three of the ten sections of the law were passed, leaving seven sections for future legislation. Now, more than twenty years later, significant gaps still exist between what the law intended to accomplish and what is currently implemented and useful. Even so, in the brief time we were there, it felt as though the tiny Middle Eastern country had figured out accessibility pretty well.

Their flagship airline, EL AL, however, was an altogether different story.

At first glance, the brand-new 787-900 Dreamliner was stunning. It appeared impeccably designed, every amenity and detail carefully thought out. I had opted for business class, figuring the eleven-hour flight would suck that much less with more room in and around the seats to help me do whatever I needed.

Having already flown as a "passenger with special needs" a few times on shorter trips, I was almost used to the boarding rigmarole. Flag down airport staff. Explain that you're not walking anywhere, no how, no way, not even a little. Ignore looks of disgust. Roll to the gate and board first in that dreadful category "Anyone Needing Extra Time to Board." And then roll to the end of the jet bridge to the dreaded aisle chair.

This child-sized chair is loaded with straps, buckles, and harnesses to ensure you don't escape. It looks and feels like a medieval torture device. It also comes with plenty of stares from onlookers. The more ambitious airport staff will pick you up and transfer you to the chair. Those not interested in the impending slipped disc will let you figure out the transfer for yourself.

Once in the chair, you're snaked down the aisle toward your row. In most planes, you're rolled next to your seat and more or less transferred out of the chair the same way you were transferred into it. The rows in EL AL's business class are arranged in a different, one-two-one seat configuration, each seat designed as a full bedroom, kitchen, and entertainment center. All the comforts of home and then some, except for the paltry eighteen inches of space separating the rows—barely enough room to shuffle sideways, let alone maneuver a disabled person into a seat.

After unshackling me from the torture-chamber chair, two surly flight attendants, with direction and help from my father, placed me into the seat. *Bring the booze, stat!*

During the planning for this trip, we spent a lot of time on the topic of going to the bathroom. I had attempted to work out the maximum amount I could drink without having to take a piss—

based on the volume of the human bladder divided by the duration of the flight time. It was mind over bladder, and I was determined to win. The alternative was one of those pee bags strapped to my leg for the duration of the flight. Wanting to steer clear of that option, we decided to go bag-free and figure it out midflight. We carried my walker on board and planned to use it to assist me down the aisle to the bathroom and back.

About six hours into the trip, the inevitable happened. No amount of squirming, repositioning, or attempting to sleep was going to make the urge to urinate go away. My father and I spent several minutes working out the logistics of navigating to the bathroom. It was no more than fifteen feet in front of us, but this was going to be difficult. What we hadn't accounted for were the ultra-narrow aisles, the unreasonably small bathroom doorway, and the lack of assistive items that I depended on being in place. As nice as the plane decor was, it was disability unusable.

Adding to the urgency of the situation was the complex navigation out of my seat, which required shuffling awkwardly past the seat on my left and toward the bathroom. My father turned on his commander mode to ensure the two flight attendants he enlisted to help support this endeavor were in sync. This was going to be more complex than the choreography of a Cirque du Soleil show.

My father held me up on the left, two muscular flight attendants took my weight on my right, and we were on the move. Once I was liberated from the beautiful cocoon-like seat pods, a walker was placed in front of me, necessary for stability. One awkward step at a time, we traversed our way toward the front of the cabin.

Once we arrived at the bathroom, the next set of logistics was debated and enacted: turn left, enter the coat closet–sized bathroom stall, and position myself over the toilet. How? We opted for brute force. Awkward, but effective. We got the job done without spilling a drop.

What the airline lacked in design accommodations, they made

up for in their business-class amenities. The luxurious travel gift set, the fluffy socks, the endless supply of food and booze, the nonstop movies. And, oh, the beautiful flight attendants. (Check Instagram if you don't believe me). Of course, they're also Israeli, so you know they've been in the army, and they can probably kill you!

When it came time to eat, my mother situated herself in the cavernous pod and adjusted my plates to begin cutting my food and feeding me. The configuration of the seats isn't conducive to this particular activity, or to a few others that come to mind, but we were managing.

Noticing that we were slow to make our way through dinner, the flight attendant knelt down and asked if she could help feed me so my mother could eat her own meal. What? I never get this level of service in top-tier restaurants, not to mention in any class cabin on an airplane where the waitress also happens to be a highly trained flight attendant responsible for hundreds of lives.

Heartened by the travel elements that worked well, I was eager to take on my next excursion. Denver has always been one of my favorite cities for many reasons—the crisp, clean air, the big outdoors culture, the stunning scenery, and the laid-back feeling, to name a few. The ever-present and very legal marijuana doesn't hurt either.

Since the beginning of my ALS journey, I've been on a mission to find something, anything that would alleviate my symptoms. While waiting for my medical marijuana card to arrive, I needed immediate relief, so what better place to visit than mile-high Denver?

It's a fairly accessible city, and with the widespread use of ride-sharing apps like Uber, I was excited about the trip. As always, my visit was well planned for ease of getting around.

But when the first Uber driver pulled up in an SUV, a barrage of questions flooded my mind: How high is that seat and just how do I get up there? Is the door handle in the right spot? Are my weakening hands still strong enough to grab something and prevent me from hitting the ground? If the seats aren't leather, will I be able to slide myself into place? And then after the drive, how do I ease myself down?

About a year before, Uber had installed a supposedly compassionate and customer-centric CEO. TV ads touted that the safety and comfort of passengers was the company's new top priority. I figured now would be a good time to reach out to them for help in finding vehicles that better suited my needs. After all, I can choose the luxury level and size of the vehicle I want to be picked up in, so why not the accessibility?

Nowhere in the Uber app was I able to indicate my special needs. I emailed customer service hoping they would offer a solution I hadn't explored. Instead, two days later, I got a cheery, yet dismissive email that basically said I couldn't specifically request a sedan. If one didn't show up when I booked a ride, I could just cancel and start over.

They couldn't be serious. As if it were fine and dandy for me to wait for a driver two times (or more) because I was disabled.

Uber tracks millions of data points to provide a highly customized experience for riders and drivers. Why not disability needs? The airline industry has allowed its passengers to do this for years—where you want to sit, the type of food you want, and, of course, whether or not you need "special assistance."

Compounding that frustration are the drivers, who must carry their fair share of responsibility in behaving like human beings. Star rating isn't the only metric they are judged by. They're also evaluated by the number of complaints filed against them and even the frequency with which they turn down rides in undesirable areas. This type of profiling is completely acceptable.

Come to find out, I wasn't the only one getting one-star service. On June 11, 2019, the Disability Rights Advocates (DRA) and the law firm Carlson Lynch filed a class action lawsuit against Uber. According to the DRA website, the suit alleges that "Uber fails to provide any wheelchair accessible vehicles through its on-demand ride-sharing service in Pittsburgh."

The DRA has since filed similar suits against Uber in New York and California.

9

Weed Does a Body Good

"I want a goddamn strong statement on marijuana . . . I want to hit it, against legalizing and all that sort of thing."
—Richard Nixon

I HAVE A LOVE-HATE RELATIONSHIP with the idea of marijuana. I grew up during Ronald Reagan's "War on Drugs" and the torrent of anti-drug public service announcements intended to scare everyone (but didn't). One TV ad shows a guy in a kitchen holding an egg in his hand. "This is your brain," he says. Then he points to a sizzling frying pan. "This is drugs." He cracks the egg into the pan and says, "This is your brain on drugs. Any questions?"

Yes, actually. Can I get that sunny side up with a side of hash browns?

My all-time favorite commercial: a father walks into his son's bedroom holding a small cigar box full of drugs and drug paraphernalia. "Your mother found this in your closet," the father barks at him. "Where did you get it?"

The son starts to speak, but the father interrupts him. "Who taught you how to do this stuff?"

The son fires back, "You, all right? I learned it by watching you."

Where exactly was this kid's father doing drugs so his son could see him? More importantly, the dad should have been pleased his kid had his own stash and kept his hands off his own OG Kush.

The war on drugs also created the D.A.R.E. program (Drug Abuse Resistance Education). The powers that be decided it would be smart to introduce this program to the school kids through local law enforcement. That way, the kids would think the cops were their buddies and wouldn't have a problem narking on their friends who just wanted to get high behind the bleachers.

I was never opposed to recreational marijuana—I just had no use for it. In college and then later in NYC, it was a way of life. What was probably closer to the truth was that I was simply oblivious.

I tried marijuana for the first time in Miami while visiting my buddy Ido and his girlfriend Jennifer. The plan was to have a nice dinner, return to Ido's place where I was staying, watch a movie, and call it a night. Before we left the house, Jennifer brought out an edible gummy that she promised was "no big deal." She cut it into quarters, offered one to Ido and me, skipped herself since she was driving, and wrapped up the remaining pieces.

Before I popped the miniscule, squishy red candy cube into my mouth, I took a survey of the situation at hand. I was in good company and we were going to a restaurant that had stellar reviews. What could possibly go wrong?

By the time dinner was served, I had all but forgotten about the tiny gummy. Red wine, house-made burrata, and shrimp cargot accompanied by warm crusty bread. But then things went sideways. Feeling a bit nauseated, I announced to the table it would be in everyone's best interest to point me in the direction of the bathroom so I could curl up and die next to the bowl. Jennifer convinced me I was fine, and it was probably the four pounds of cheese I had just consumed.

As I wavered between nausea and extreme hysterics, we finished the meal and got up to leave. Maybe we were asked to leave. I don't recall. What I still see clearly is the football field distance between our table and the exit. Rising to my feet, I felt the full effect of the gummy. My body felt like a marshmallow, in a good way. There was just one problem—if I let go of the table, I would surely fall off the planet. Hanging on to Ido's shoulder to guide me out of the restaurant, I somehow made it back to the car.

When we got home, time seemed to stand still. Every movement took forever to accomplish. Ido left, saying he was taking his dog for a walk. Where did he go? If he felt anything like I did, how was he getting home? The world had become one giant mystery.

I attempted to logic my way out of the situation using my now mushy brain to calculate how much longer I would be in this predicament. If you take the weight of weed in the gummy, factor how much food I had eaten and over what period of time, subtract my body weight, and divide it by an even number—because dividing by an odd number was too difficult—I would come up with . . . bupkis.

Fuck it. Might as well enjoy it.

Fortunately, I came out the other side unscathed. All in all, it was an enjoyable experience, though not worth turning into a habit, especially if I wanted to be a functional human being.

If you like getting high, be honest with yourself and everyone else and just admit it. No need to hide behind the health benefits as the reason you sneak a joint between meetings. No one will fault you for gobbling down half a gummy to make your annoying kids a little more tolerable.

(Same rationale for gun owners. No one is going to call you or your neighbors to form a militia, your home isn't being invaded, and the government isn't coming to take your precious guns away. You'll save yourself a lot of time and effort in what will most likely be factually inaccurate arguments if you just admit it: you like guns.)

When I went to Denver on my weed-buying mission, the objective was simple.

Visit a bunch of dispensaries, buy a fistful of edibles, and try them all to see what could alleviate my symptoms. But how do you look for such places? Some stoners had at least one brilliant idea between bong rips: Leafly, a website that lists all medical and recreational marijuana dispensaries across the country. And for your smoking pleasure, they have a convenient app to help you locate the dispensary nearest to you. Four dispensaries were within a few blocks of my hotel, so I set out to find them and learn as much as I could.

For an industry that's all about "compassionate care," I was surprised to discover that most locations weren't accessible. Plus, they didn't have low counters to allow someone in a wheelchair to easily interact with the person behind the counter. Though the dispensaries offer all kinds of edibles, tinctures, and even suppositories, if you want the old-school bud and your hands don't work, you're out of luck. The majority of the devices designed to consume weed require a considerable amount of dexterity to operate.

Those nuisances aside, I got quite an education. This is some scientific shit, man. No longer do you need to rely on your dealer to bring you whatever weed he might have received from the mule that supplied him. You can walk into a dispensary, look over an extensive menu of options, and decide what kind of experience you want.

I was under the impression that weed was weed. Quite the contrary.

With the exception of a small handful of dispensary employees I met, most were willing to spend as much time as I wanted schooling me on the considerable range of products available at their store. The "budtenders" as they referred to themselves, had an impressive knowledge of all things cannabis. They must have gone to weed college. It was like I had accidentally walked into graduate-level honors advanced biology class, in Greek.

Questions about the type of experience and blend ratios and session expectations were hurled at me. Hang on a minute, Cheech. I have muscle spasms, anxiety, and a healthy dose of depression.

Gimme something to take that all away. And I want to be calm, not comatose. Think you can help me with that?

At a high level, there are really only two things to consider: Indica versus sativa and THC versus CBD (tetrahydrocannabinol versus cannabidiol). All the available choices are simply different combinations of those four components. For example, if you want something to help you sleep, go heavier with an indica that contains more THC. Want something to help you make it through another insufferable meeting where you know you'll be called on? Stick to a sativa that's heavier on CBD.

I'll probably get slammed by weed aficionados for oversimplifying this, but for the purposes of venturing into the wide world of weed, it isn't that hard.

"But Jeremy, aren't you a coffee lover?" my friends would say. "Isn't the coffee universe just as complex? How could you simplify the complexities of that special plant and all it offers?"

Sure, there are all sorts of coffees from around the world and an equally dizzying array of methods of preparing the sweet brown goodness. But for most people just venturing into their first few cups, they need to know about just two types: good coffee and the shit served in hotel lobbies. Keep it simple.

With a few exceptions, I was pointed in the right direction toward CBD-heavy strains and edibles. Concerned that I was going to end up a blithering idiot barely able to hang on to the world, I asked for some operating guidelines for the edibles:

- Do take a small amount at first.
- Don't take another until an hour has passed and you can judge the effects.
- Do make sure you're in good company.
- Don't assume you'll be a functional human being.
- Do expect the effects to last for a few hours.
- Don't wait until you're high to order food.

- Do have some of your favorite snacks within easy reach.
- Finally, don't panic—it's just weed. No one has ever died from it.

The last few rules about food are a cautionary reminder to myself after one of my friends in NYC got high, ordered an astonishing amount of Chinese food, and promptly passed out, leaving it all with the doorman. Funny the first time, but highly concerning after the third.

Today I use several types of marijuana every day depending on my body's complaints. According to the experts, it can provide all sorts of different medical benefits. My unscientific evaluation done over an extremely short time concludes that weed causes relaxation. Regardless of what body part or symptom, it will become relaxed.

If you have never tried cannabis, please apply a willing suspension of disbelief. This marvelous stuff helps me with all sorts of nasty symptoms, like muscle cramping, fasciculations (those twitches you can see on my skin), clonus of my feet and jaw (repetitive shaking, similar to teeth chattering when it's cold), excessive saliva, and insomnia. As a happy, seemingly obvious secondary benefit, weed has alleviated my anxiety and depression. That makes perfect sense, right? If you don't feel lousy, you're not going to be depressed.

Lastly, it removes the "fucks," as in who gives a fuck. Surprisingly, no matter how many fucks you have or believe you're supposed to have, weed eliminates all traces of them. If your rabbi, childhood hero, or even your boss demands you have a healthy quantity of them on hand to give, the quiet little plant with all its complexities will ensure you're free of them. After all I endured, I finally found a way to give zero fucks.

The US government classified marijuana as a Schedule I drug under the Controlled Substances Act of 1970 as part of "an international movement to wipe the cannabis plant off the face of the earth." This classification has remained ever since. All the drugs in that category, including heroin, LSD, and peyote, are defined as having "no currently accepted medical use and a high potential for abuse."

The 1970 Act was the heaviest blow to the proliferation of cannabis in the modern day—fifty years ago. Prior to that, increased restrictions and labeling of cannabis as a poison began in many states from 1906 onward, moving to outright prohibitions in the 1920s. By the mid-1930s, cannabis was regulated as an illicit drug in every state.

As of the end of 2021, thirty-nine states, including Washington, DC, have legalized medical marijuana, eighteen of which have legalized it for recreational purposes. This is progress, but we still have a long way to go.

Medical research involving marijuana has been restricted for many years in the United States due to the classification. Finally, in 2001, the Food and Drug Administration (FDA) announced approval of Epidiolex, the first-ever cannabidiol-based drug for treating two rare forms of epilepsy.

This paved the way for approval of three synthetic cannabis-related drug products: Marinol and Syndros (both also known as Dronabinol) and Cesamet (Nabilone). But the FDA, in its infinitesimal wisdom, didn't approve applications to market these drugs. So chances are your doctor is unaware of these drugs. If they are familiar, your doctor is probably too scared to prescribe or recommend them.

Every biotech company wants to get in on the action, hoping they will find the next cannabis-derived blockbuster drug. This is evidenced by a quick search on ClinicalTrials.gov for cannabis-related clinical trials. A whopping 350 trials are at various stages in the United States at the time this book was written. Of those, 207 have been completed (only 87 with results), 120 are active, and

23 aren't active. Although a high number of clinical trials focus on marijuana, the United States has been struggling to get high-quality plants for research in sufficient quantities, causing the trials to languish.

This serious deficit in quality was brought to light by Dr. Sue Sisley, who heads the Scottsdale Research Institute in Arizona. Today, the federal government has licensed only one facility to grow and supply marijuana for research purposes: the University of Mississippi. Dr. Sisley believes the cannabis that the university "disseminates to other researchers is low-quality, which could detrimentally impact their research."

When she examined the study material she received, it appeared to be full of leaves and twigs, nothing close to the quality found in dispensaries around the country. It's no wonder the results from the trials that do make it past the excruciating application process rarely yield halfway decent results.

Dr. Sisley sued the FDA and won, at least partially. "While the attorneys got the relief that they were seeking from the DEA, they interpret the 'rule making' process as the Federal agencies' code word for 'delay strategy,'" she said. "This is definitely not a full victory until we see real world cannabis flower finally being used in FDA-controlled clinical trials."

Since moving back to my childhood home, I've introduced many new things into my parents' lives. Restaurants, music, technology (at severe heartache to all of us)—and, of course, marijuana. Depending on their ailment, I've suggested a little dab of CBD ointment or a few tiny puffs on the vaporizer pen. They saw how my symptoms improved when I used the different forms, so they were willing to try it.

My parents have endured tremendous stress and strain in their lives by taking care of me during what was supposed to be their golden years. Feeling a bit like an enabler, I wanted my parents to relax and maybe laugh their heads off over nothing and everything at the same time.

Far be it from me to coerce anyone into doing something they don't want to do. Without making my parents nonfunctional, I wanted to be a good steward of the holy plant and guide them through their first experience. "Take a couple of puffs," I told them. "Don't suck it down too hard, and breathe out."

The first question from my father: "Am I high yet?"

Spoken like the true scientist he is, he wanted to analyze everything that was happening and predict what would come next.

"How would I know?" I said. "It's weed. Sit down and try to enjoy yourself."

Though neither of my parents felt any immediate effects, both of them slept better than they had in years. Even more, they had no arthritis pain when they woke up.

I'm hoping that weed becomes a gateway drug for them, but not in a huddled-next-to-a-dumpster-behind-the-7-Eleven-popping-out-each-other's-gold-fillings-to-buy-another-hit-of-crack kind of way. Let's call it a positive gateway to more life experiences.

Consider your own parents and how much more relaxed they might be with a little weed. Hell, it was their generation who wrote "Puff the Magic Dragon" and sang about "Momma's Little Helper." Maybe if the stars align, I'll hotbox the van on our next family trip and get my father high enough to convince him to purchase a non-flip phone. The moral of the story here is that you're never too old for peer pressure.

In this house, a pinch of Sour Diesel can help us conquer all the new challenges we're facing on a daily basis, like the Apple TV remote, which looks the same whether it's upside down or right side up. Or one of my vape pens, which requires multiple clicks to turn on, heat, and draw from. Or my iPhone X, which sucks to use, irrespective of your dexterity and technology savviness.

Imagine my frustratingly limited ability to teach my parents how to operate these devices with my inability to speak, curled fingers that point to nowhere helpful, and general impatience for these types of efforts.

Weed does my body good.

10

In Sickness and in Health

WHAT WOULD YOU DO IF your spouse became terminally ill?

A. Stand by your spouse's side?
B. Run for the hills?

I hope you never have to face that situation, though it's a real possibility. You may think, *Of course I would do anything for my sweetheart*—a logical and emotionally sane thought, considering your marriage vows committed you two for better or worse, in sickness and in health. You're also probably thinking, *That will never happen to me.*

Close your eyes for a moment and envision the life you dreamed of, the life you have worked hard to achieve. Do you see the big house in the burbs with lots of kids running around? Or a massive loft apartment in the middle of downtown? Are your closest friends gathered in the kitchen sharing wine and laughing at stories? Are you entertaining other families, showing off your perfect life? Surrounding yourself with the finer things life has to offer? Or maybe exploring the world?

Now add in one part mysterious symptoms, two parts fear, and a dash of anxiety, and bring it all to boil for six to twelve months, and you have yourself the makings of a dream-killing, relationship-straining disaster soup. As everything simmers, the rising scent of something more serious fills the air. Could it be MS (multiple sclerosis), ALS, or any number of other diseases requiring an acronym?

Going down the WebMD rabbit hole, where every itch and cough immediately leads to flesh-eating zombie cancer, will transform your beautiful fairy-tale dreams to a life filled with doctor appointments, therapies of all sorts, nurses and aides in and out of the house, enough medical equipment to fill a small hospital—and a mountain of bills.

Anyone faced with something of this magnitude will have their mental and physical strength pushed to the limits. The strength of the bond between you and your significant other is also tested as both of you receive the diagnosis, even though only one of you is sick.

Ask yourself: What are you prepared to do? It's a good idea to answer this question for yourself *before* you get married.

By the time I started this journey, my wife and I had been married for a year and a half. We were living in NYC, along with her two-pound teacup Yorkie, in a five-hundred-square-foot apartment in midtown east near the United Nations. Cramped doesn't even begin to describe how it felt to live in a well-appointed, though excessively furnished, junior one-bedroom.

On top of that, we both worked from home full time. The gym in the basement of our building provided the added benefit of an extra toilet and shower.

To illustrate just how small our place was, a colleague and good friend of mine won an award and received a bottle of wine as a prize. Because he needed to fly home, he asked me to keep the wine until he could drive into the city and pick it up. I was only too willing to help him but I simply didn't have the space in my apartment. Yes, seriously. Living in NYC, we learned to use every last square inch available to us.

I often gave us a break from ourselves when I left to visit clients for work. Not wanting to be away from home more than necessary, I pushed to come home every night regardless of how far I traveled. Day trips from New York to Dallas and Jacksonville weren't uncommon.

As the terrifying medical mystery took over my life, I experienced frequent, unfamiliar changes. Managing them wasn't as simple as going to the CVS on the corner and grabbing something from the shelf. It was nearly impossible to determine what equipment or medication I needed before a new symptom reared its ugly head and I would need something else to help me in a different way.

Being independent by nature and not wanting to burden my wife, I didn't ask for help at first, convincing myself that the symptoms were of no real consequence and I could deal with them on my own. That quickly changed as I got worse and struggled with basic everyday tasks, like getting on and off the couch, opening bottles, and dressing myself.

But my wife's proactive help, which I so desperately needed, never came.

Working full time, along with attempting to identify an unknown disease, managing the symptoms, going to never-ending doctor appointments, and doing my best to keep a happy household, was more than I could bear. I became short-tempered, anxious, and depressed.

The emotional distance between us grew and communication broke down. As I frantically searched for answers, she pulled away from me and from anything having to do with my illness. I can only assume that the crushing weight of what she was watching her husband go through was preventing her from openly sharing her feelings with me, or the people closest to her. The weeks and months flew by, and I felt more alone than I ever had in my life.

The walls of our apartment began to close in on us. Our tiny dog was nearing thirteen years old and needing more help getting around, while our beautifully decorated apartment became a maze of sharp corners, reminding me each time I fell. We had no room to store the growing number of medical supplies, and the apartment my wife once considered her safe space was being overrun by a nightmare neither of us could escape.

If we were going to make it through together unscathed, we needed a larger place and more help with every aspect of our lives. So I started looking for all sorts of alternative living arrangements in and around the city. The apartment rental industry is scummy, filled with bait-and-switch scams, unscrupulous and uncaring agents, and a plethora of overpriced concrete filth boxes that you wouldn't subject your worst enemy to.

I combed through all the rental listing sites for key terms that would accommodate our needs, like ADA-compliant accessibility, roll-in showers, grab handles, and elevators. My efforts yielded very little. Reaching out to the buildings directly proved useless as well. Many places claimed to be ADA compliant, though upon further investigation, they were neither accessible nor usable. Not a single person I spoke with had knowledge of or access to an apartment that could accommodate my needs.

I was silently being told, "Fuck you, we don't want your kind here."

The urgency and anxiety increased with every day. Hit the panic button. *Where do we go? Will my symptoms stay stable long enough for us to find another place to live?* Not wanting to alarm my company, I kept my condition to myself as long as I could.

Deep down, I believe my wife shared in my fear and panic, though I was never certain. She continued to take refuge from the crumbling reality around her through marijuana, endless hours of video games, and silence. Entire evenings passed without a twitch of movement from the couch where she was perched. I wished with all my heart that I could feel the warmth of her embrace to calm my trembling hands and frequent fits of tear-filled grief. That wish would never be fulfilled.

Where there were questions, I frantically sought answers, sharing the results of every search. Exasperated and needing a partner to brainstorm with, I often felt dismissed in favor of more games of Candy Crush and another joint. I ached to break down her barriers and tell her that everything would be all right as long as we had each other.

Not long after I returned from the Mayo Clinic with the devastating diagnosis, we started couples therapy. I was looking for anything that would make our lives even slightly better, but I learned she was looking for something else. She made it clear that she couldn't—and wouldn't—become my primary caregiver, saying that I should live with my parents. This wasn't simply a suggestion—it was her objective.

The next kick in the gut came a couple of weeks later. In the therapist's office, she turned to me and said she was done. She wanted a divorce.

The woman I had hoped to spend the rest of my life with was running away at the most difficult time in our lives. In June 2018 I had no choice but to move back to my parents' house, into a supportive and loving environment where I could focus on my health.

But she lied. She wasn't done. It wasn't enough for her to shatter my heart. She had to stomp on it too.

She dragged out the divorce, leveraging my failing health as an opportunity to extort as much out of me as she could. Through her sociopathic lack of empathy and baseless sense of entitlement, she made every effort to cause crippling stress. What she extolled as a simple prenup created a nonsensical mess that multiple lawyers would curse.

If she wanted to wash her hands of me, why did she do that? No moral compass? Her family, especially her father, would be ashamed if they knew how she had treated me. She had surprised us all by figuring out a way to profit from my ALS.

There were no visits to see how I was doing, no get-well cards, no offers to come cheer me up, only the occasional communication from her lawyer adding to the growing list of demands that she would drag on for more than a year.

Message received: I was only worthwhile in health and in wealth.

Yimakh shemo ve zikhro. (May her name and memory be erased.)

There's an important distinction between *getting* married and *being* married. At the risk of sounding like a misogynistic asshole and utterly insensitive to the fairer sex, my experiences have taught me that women, more so than men, fall victim to idealizing the getting-married half of the equation without taking a sufficiently critical look inward to determine whether they are prepared for a relationship lasting the rest of their lives.

After you come back from your romantic honeymoon and finish putting away all the gifts and writing thank-yous, it's time to shift gears to *being* married. This is when shit gets real. The postnuptial shifts that newlyweds experience aren't always obvious, so it's important to pay extra close attention.

Communication changes. It's no longer sufficient to sit passively and expect your spouse to make all the decisions after reading your mind for what you want to eat for dinner, watch on television, and do over the weekend. It's an infuriating game that might have been cute during courtship but shouldn't last long after the honeymoon.

Sex changes. Chances are you have already used up the two porn moves you knew when you first started dating. Now it's a race to each other's magic pleasure buttons so you can get the act over with and get back to the *Shitty Housewives of Some Town* marathon you interrupted for the mandatory Missionary Wednesday's obligation. Slow down, take your time, and appreciate each other.

Roles and responsibilities harden. Taking out the garbage isn't worth arguing about. And your subpar free-throw skills will never earn you a nomination into the Hamper Hall of Fame. I promise you, she might have thought that was cute once or twice, but she's now dreaming of ways to murder you in your sleep with that crusty pair of briefs.

The responsibilities in your life aren't going away. In fact, they will compound over time and become more complex, having greater impact. Talk to each other about what you're comfortable doing and what you're not. If you can't figure out the adult Tetris necessary to load the dishwasher to maximize space, I might offer to take that responsibility. Similarly, if you don't like the new colors I've made your favorite white blouse in the wash, feel free to declare yourself Master of the Laundry.

Decisions become permanent and affect more than you alone. During bachelorhood, it was perfectly acceptable to stay out all hours, blow half the rent on a bottle at the club, and eat take-out every night. But once you're married, or at least cohabitating seriously, it's time to start looking out for each other.

I asked one of my closest female friends what she would do if her spouse became terminally ill. It wasn't the difficult carê that bothered her, nor was it the death of the dreams of the perfect life. She said a "conversation would need to happen" about sex, and that she would have to get her needs met outside the relationship. I was hurt and saddened to hear this.

Was it possible that I expected too much from my partner in a relationship? More probable was that I was no longer a viable provider, either financially or sexually, and a new and more capable partner had to be found. In my declining condition, I had become invisible to my wife.

• • •

But as they say, when one door closes, another one opens.

On a Saturday afternoon, amid all the darkness of my diagnosis and divorce, an old, familiar name popped up on my phone.

Melissa and I had met about ten years before in Sag Harbor. We both knew someone who knew someone who invited us to a boozy summer weekend in the Hamptons. While the name "Hamptons" generally conjures up an air of sophistication and refinement, the accommodations could only be described as a flophouse—more like the seedy Jersey Shore than the glamorous Hamptons.

After I spotted Melissa across the room and started talking to her, we were inseparable the rest of the weekend. How could I resist the beautiful blond with a snarky sense of humor that mirrored my own? Soon after, we started dating.

We went on trips together, hitting the slopes in Vermont, Melissa with her skis and me with my board. The following spring, we spent a weekend in DC at the cherry blossom festival, climbing the large, beautiful trees like little kids and taking silly tourist photos on the mall. On Sunday afternoon, we had high tea at a swanky hotel before heading back to New York.

A year and a half later, I lost my mind and broke up with her. What was up with that? A mixture of immaturity and grass-is-greener thinking, I suspect. Lucky for me, we stayed friends, but our calls tapered off when I got married.

Now Melissa was reaching out to me. Her timing couldn't have been better. I needed her friendship and kindness. We talked about her life, my diagnosis, my failed marriage. We talked about everything and anything—and all the old joking and humor returned.

She and I started texting back and forth every day, and then we made plans to meet, though I put it off a few times. I was nervous about her seeing how much I had changed, expecting her to run for the hills. She met me at an infusion clinic where I was getting one of my anti-ALS potions intravenously (it didn't help), alongside all the Upper East Side housewives with fibromyalgia.

After the treatment, Melissa helped me out of the chair and to my crutches. We grabbed lunch at the sandwich shop below the clinic, requiring the least amount of my now-awkward Bambi-on-ice walking. As soon as we sat down, we fell into an easy conversation, reminiscing and laughing.

When the bill came, I couldn't resist turning my dexterity problems into the ultimate icebreaker. "I'm not trying to be fresh, but can you get my wallet from my front pocket?"

With a sly grin, she slid her hand into my pants, and, well, that rekindled our relationship. ALS attacks the motor neurons responsible for voluntary muscle movement, but happily, it doesn't affect voluntary muscles or sexual arousal. Still, my divorce, coupled with my worsening symptoms, made me think that physical intimacy was over for me.

I never even considered that I could love or be loved again. Of course, I wanted it, but I couldn't let myself think it was possible. And how could I put Melissa through such a difficult existence?

"Jer," she often says to me, "I'd rather cram a lifetime into the time we have left than to spend a day without you in it." If she could, she would figure out a way to love the ALS out of me.

When Melissa and I first reconnected, she was working in hospitality management, but after learning more about ALS and experimental treatments, she landed a job in Boston working on a clinical trial therapy for the disease. She still managed to drive back and forth to my parents' house in New Jersey on the weekends. When Sunday came around, I would wish for more Saturdays. I was forever worried about her driving in the dark, snow, or rain, and would kick her out of the house early depending on the forecast.

One weekend the following spring, Melissa packed up the van and hauled us back to Washington DC, though not for the cherry blossom festival this time. We may or may not have told my parents that we were doing the traditional sight-seeing, but we actually went to a convention that was for, shall we say, a sexually inclusive community. The wheelchair I'm confined to, usually a barrier, was hardly noticed in this setting. In fact, I seemed quite vanilla compared to many of the others' proclivities.

We attended several of the classes on intimacy with disabilities. The experience was like buying a porn magazine and reading the articles, but the information was useful, complete with detailed demonstrations. While a certain amount of creativity is required, it was nice to be in an environment where intimacy with disability was normalized.

At the end of the weekend, Melissa drove us back to New Jersey, and by the time we turned into our neighborhood, it was dark. She slowed and then stopped the car about a block or two away from the house.

That was peculiar. How could she drive all the way from DC only to get lost a block away from the house? I was about to provide her with "keep driving straight" directions, when she leaned over and kissed me. She wanted the weekend to last a few moments longer, she said, and pretend that we were simply two people coming back home from a date weekend. If ever I could pause ALS and hold a moment forever . . .

In early 2020, Melissa moved in with us and landed a job in cancer therapies at nearby Bristol Myers Squibb. She is the light of my life, a selfless partner and friend who doesn't need anything from me but my presence.

This journey is teaching me that love comes in many different forms from many different directions. I've received a gift I never believed was truly achievable—unconditional acceptance.

With each passing day, I think about what could have been if I had been a smarter man all those years ago.

11

Cab Driver as Spiritual Diagnostician

COMING OUT OF A DOCTOR'S appointment on a cold Thursday evening in Manhattan, I stepped into the street to hail a cab. I was still using forearm crutches then, and I raised one in the air toward a cab whose roof light was on, signaling it was available.

It was one of the new taxi vans the city had just deployed, advertised for exceptional accessibility, but another case of the designer not consulting with the end user. The heavy sliding door is more fitting for a bank vault than for an accessible taxi, and oddly, the entry step is high. If you have mobility or height challenges, this taxi isn't for you.

Every time I see one of those vans, I envision a modern-day Norman Rockwell painting of a plump old lady in a house dress, with uneven knee-high stockings and purply-bluish cotton puffs of white hair, struggling to get into this monster vehicle, two of her grandchildren pushing her from behind.

Still, I muscled my way into the cab, gave the address, and fired up my phone, intent on finding any distraction from this life that I could. But the cab driver interrupted my search. "It looks like you have a problem with your leg," he said with a thick Jamaican accent.

No shit, Sherlock. All I wanted to do was play the little game on my phone in silence on the way to see my friends at Black Tap restaurant, known for obscenely large and diabetes-inducing milkshakes.

There's an unspoken rule governing the interaction between the cab driver and the passenger: Don't speak to each other, and the ride will be much more pleasant for both of you.

But he continued on. "It's actually a neurological problem."

Okay, he got my attention. "How do you know?"

"I felt it through my whole body when you got into the cab."

That was incredible. I'd been to so many doctors and had hundreds of tests. Why hadn't I saved myself a ton of time and energy and just gotten into this guy's cab?

"Did you hurt someone in your past?"

I'm a pretty stand-up guy. I don't go out looking for a fight. I vote. I pay my taxes. And at that time, I had a respectable job and called my parents once a week.

"Not physically," he said. "Emotionally or spiritually."

Now that was a different story. Thinking this guy had all the answers, I asked the next logical question, "What should I do?"

"I don't know, but the answer lies in the spiritual side."

"Okay, I'm on it."

After pondering our conversation for a couple of days, I came up with a two-pronged approach. I'd begin by reaching out to my friends and family members involved with spirituality of some sort. One friend is deep into Kabbalah, another friend swears by inspirational YouTube videos, and my father's side of the family is Jewish orthodox. Surely someone had to know what this guy was talking about and how I could tap into it.

At the same time, I kicked off the 2018 Jeremy Apology Tour. I thought back long and hard about all the people I might have hurt in one way or another. Friends, ex-girlfriends, relatives, old coworkers. I came up with a list and wrote emails or Facebook Messenger messages to everyone. I don't know whether this is what that cab driver had in mind, but it felt good, addressed a lot of deep-down feelings, and eliminated some of my anxiety.

A little over a month later, coming out of the same doctor's office at around the same time, I got into a cab and heard from the front, "Do you remember me? You didn't do what I told you to do."

I leaned over so I could look through the partition and see the face attached to the familiar voice. What were the odds? Pretty good, apparently.

"What do I do now?" I asked.

"Pray," he said. "Whatever religion you are, whatever God you believe in, you should pray."

That was something I had never done before. But this guy had shown up in my life for a reason, and I decided I should sit up and listen. After all, I wasn't getting any better.

When I told this story to one of my friends, she introduced me to a guy named Robert, a "master healer," whatever that meant. I figured he was going to wave some crystals at me, take my money, and tell me I should try twice more. If I didn't like the experience, or didn't get anything out of it, at least I would have tried.

Unlike a majority of Western physicians, alternative medicine practitioners don't accept health insurance, which means they don't have to run their practice like a factory churning through another patient every twelve minutes. They can spend considerable time listening to understand the ailments completely, so ideally, they can choose the appropriate crystals, locations to place the acupuncture needles, or elixirs and tree bark to compound.

What's more likely is that they are compiling the best sales pitch possible that leaves the patient hopeful and protects them in case their treatment fails.

I was desperate to put a halt to whatever was happening to me, and I saw no harm in trying something new. With an open mind, I made an appointment with Robert and met him at his midtown Manhattan office. Expecting to see someone dressed in gypsy clothes, like the women with a folding table and tarot cards sitting on the sidewalk, I was surprised. He was a slightly disheveled, five-foot-seven, sixty-something gray-haired man wearing ill-fitting jeans, what looked like a filthy sweater, and twisted gym socks.

He came shuffling down the carpeted hallway and motioned for me to follow him. With space in Manhattan at such a premium, I was prepared for a small office, but not the tiny nine-by-six room crammed with a desk, examination table, and two chairs. He asked me if we could embrace to say hello, a first for me in a setting like that. But I had gone in with an open mind, so if he told me that riding an ostrich in nothing but my boots down Fifth Avenue was going to help, I would have done it.

After about forty minutes talking about the practice of healing, my goals, and what to expect, it was time to begin. With difficulty and much assistance, I lay on his examination table. The fifteen-minute session consisted of incense, chanting, and some gentle, appropriate touching. The only odd experiences I had during the session were a feeling of lightness, which could have been from the incense, and a vision of very specific memories streaming across my mind's eye from the lower left, up, and to the right, flowing like a river, each memory playing independently as it rushed by.

When his bell rang, he sat me up. I thanked him and scheduled another two sessions, willing to explore it more deeply. That night, I slept better than I had in quite a while, but after the subsequent sessions, I never experienced any further effects, either positive or negative.

Given that ALS is a neurological condition and all the symptoms are controlled by the brain, why shouldn't I be able to impart some level of control over my own squishy lump of gray matter if I tried hard enough? I wanted to find out.

I've always been drawn to meditation. Logging almost a thousand hours on my Headspace app, I practiced with the intent of learning skills should I ever need them. As the disease worsened and

I was abandoned in my own home, I used those lessons to create a mental safe space and put as much distance as possible between the man I knew I was and the symptoms taking over my body.

What started out as unnoticeable, superficial muscle twitches developed into severe nightly cramps in both calves, eventually spreading across my entire body, making sleep impossible. I would (and still do) wake up several times every night to my body begging me to change positions—but I knew how difficult the process of rolling over on my own would be.

When I had a difficult day, I counted down the hours until I could get into my warm, soft bed. It became even more of a sanctuary as I found myself needing to escape from reality. But that safe space began to crack apart once sleep would no longer allow me to hide from my symptoms.

Running to the bathroom in the middle of the night became a terrifying ordeal. Using my weakening arms and grip-less hands, I struggled to liberate myself from the covers. Then I'd get the forearm crutches, carefully stand up without falling, and shuffle around the bed, cautious not to plant a foot or crutch on the comforter. Now beeline to the bathroom. No matter how urgently I needed to piss, my body knew when I was in a rush and stiffened up and spasmed accordingly.

If I rushed, my ankles would cramp until I was forced to stand on my toes. If Lady Luck was on my side, the clonus would kick up, the uncontrollable or rhythmic shaking in my feet that made standing still a monumental task. All of this slowed the journey to the bathroom, elevating the anxiety. When I finally arrived, the choice was to either stand up to pee and risk falling over or sit down and risk not being able to get up. Either way, the constantly changing medications were making this a twice-nightly struggle.

Meditation—my in-the-moment life raft—saved me from drowning in the tsunami of whatever chemicals my brain was pumping out. With each unnatural contortion of my body, I made a conscientious effort to hear the soothing British accent of Andy Puddicombe, the voice and founder of meditation app Headspace, tell my body to soften, relax, and reset.

"Breathe in through the nose, out through the mouth. Again. Focus on the rise and fall of your stomach as you continue to breathe rhythmically."

Hang on, Jer. You're strong enough to make it through this, I would tell myself.

Each terror-filled second ticked by at a snail's pace. I tried to allow the idea of calm to wash over me and convince my body to relax so I could go on with whatever task I was struggling with at that moment.

Around the same time I began falling regularly, the anxiety started to take hold and introduced her equally sinister friend, agoraphobia. It happened in my apartment, in the doctor's office, in front of a fire station when the fire truck was coming out, and, probably the most embarrassing, on a crowded corner of Forty-Second Street and Third Avenue.

Or in the middle of the night when the sheets wrapped around me were too lightweight to grasp and pull off and they conformed around my body, constricting my movements, like being strapped to a gurney. Panic ensues . . . pulse accelerates . . . breathing shallows and quickens . . . body heat soars . . . sweat flows . . . limbs stiffen and shake. This had become a nightly ritual.

Since the panic and underlying fears were fabricated by my mind and manifesting these physical symptoms, why couldn't I outsmart my gray matter and teach it who was boss? Turns out I can—to a point. I taught myself a few techniques to prevent the anxiety from escalating, as well as showing my parents how to help at those moments. Aside from meditation, Xanax, and cannabis, how would I take control of my mind?

Maybe the cabbie was right. My afflictions were cast onto me by some deity I pissed off during a reincarnation in the Han Dynasty. Searching for God this late in the game felt a bit like feigning enthusiasm for taking your cousin as your third-place prom date choice. Everyone knows what's really going on here. Desperation makes for strange bedfellows.

I ventured into spirituality by talking to my religious cousins on my father's side. They each went to twelve years of religious day school, so among them, they should have been able to give me a Cliffs Notes version of whatever it was I needed to say or do to beat this monster. They shared websites for learning religious text with a partner, daily messages of inspiration, and versions of ancient scriptures dumbed down so I could understand the morals. But that wasn't what I was after. I needed something I could hold on to that would let me find the sunny sky amid the storm clouds.

I expanded my search, asking anyone I came across what spirituality meant to them and where I should begin. Their answers weren't helping. Most people can't articulate what spirituality means to them or how they access it in their lives. One home health aide recommended I look into the ancient art of Vodou practiced in her native Haiti. As much as my parents love me, I wasn't about to ask them to sacrifice a goat in the den.

Many in my generation have a casual relationship with religion, which is to say, almost nonexistent. At least in my social circles, people are categorically unlikely to join any organization with any real seriousness. Unlike my friend's grandparents, who enjoyed Sunday night spaghetti dinners at the VFW hall or met up with friends at the Masonic Lodge, we do none of that. Not because we believe there's no use for these types of organizations in our lives, but because we find community and support in other venues—like Facebook or at the local bar where everybody knows our name.

When I asked my Jewish friends about how a higher power fit

into their lives, the line I heard more often than not was "I'm more spiritual than religious," code for "I'll go to the high holidays if my parents buy my tickets, but that's it."

No one was giving me easy answers. Whatever it was that I was looking for was going to be found by happenstance. It's sort of like wandering around a suit store knowing only what you don't want. You may as well start on one side of the store and start trying everything on.

Several of my friends are deep into New Age spirituality in one form or another, and they seem to be doing fine. Could I find some answers there?

My close friend Erika, a yoga instructor who overflows with kindness and compassion, recommended the Eckhardt Tolle book *A New World: Awakening to Your Life's Purpose*. In 2008, the *New York Times* called Tolle "the most popular spiritual author in the United States."

Erika went into detail about how Tolle's writing inspired her and helped put her own life's questions into perspective. With such a ringing endorsement, I couldn't wait to read the book.

In the end, I didn't find a useful answer to the meaning of life, but I did find a new outlook. Simply put, it was up to me to define what my life would become. Just as I had reinvented myself when I first moved to the Big Apple, I could *choose* not to be defined by the ALS diagnosis.

Instead of living in self-pity, fear, and isolation, waiting for my time to come, I choose to . . .

- Get out of bed
- Spend my days with those who love me
- Invest in myself
- Defend my terms
- Decide how to spend my time
- Eliminate negativity

- Love unconditionally
- Wear funny T-shirts
- Listen to music
- Pay for high-quality healthcare
- Take risks
- Tear down my barriers
- Speak definitively
- Take the hard path because it's the right path
- Say yes

During Passover 2019, we went to the house of our longtime family friends Maurice and Paula. By way of tradition, Maurice, the head of the household and leader of the Seder, posed a question to those of us around the table: "Is God good or evil? And how do we know?"

Being a lifelong agnostic, I never questioned the existence of a higher power, though not in the traditional Judeo-Christian sense of God. This venture into an unforgiving disease has given me plenty of time to consider alternatives to my own belief system. I have more questions than answers, though I'm not at a loss for people offering their frequently unsolicited and, according to them, fact-based opinions. Little do they know how happy they should be that I can't speak. Then again, would they bother to listen even if they heard my opinion? Methinks not.

I'm far more inclined to believe in my own manifest destiny than in any argument supporting an unquantifiable deity having a hard-on for creating pain and suffering. Besides, I can't fathom why any god would care enough to get involved in our lives, when we have been on this planet for only a split second of its existence.

But on the off-chance that someone or something has an interest in taking action on my wishes, I've created a prayer that I say silently during any medical treatment. It goes something like this:

Please let this procedure heal me so I can take care of my parents and Melissa the way they have taken care of me.

As the anesthesia washes over me like the tide blankets a beach, I repeat this little prayer over and over. When that familiar tingle envelops my tongue and bad electronic music fills my ears, my concentration is stolen away from the prayer and any attempt to meditate, I drift off to sleep, hoping to wake up again.

12

Fundamentals of Caring

"I am the guest of honor at my own living funeral."
—Lou Gehrig during his farewell speech at
Yankees Stadium, July 4, 1939

AS TIME PASSED, THE ROUTINE at my parents' house became more refined and perfected to accommodate my rapidly changing symptoms. Living by their loving hands, I watched, wishing I could be a helpful participant, as they reengineered every step of the day to make it safe for me and easier for them.

With all the advancements in medicine and technology, there is currently no cure for ALS and no effective treatment to stop or reverse the progression of the disease. Whether I survive only long enough to fall within the statistical probability of mortality window of two to five years post-diagnosis or fight my way into becoming an outlier and living into my eighties, an existence with ALS is exhausting for patients and caregivers alike.

By my late twenties and early thirties, I had seen enough sickness and suffering to know I wanted to live life to the fullest. When I reached the bad shit-yourself-while-drooling years, I would pull the ripcord and call it quits. But having arrived at "invalid station" far earlier than expected, I'm not ready to give up.

I can handle pain. Blood, whether my own or someone else's, doesn't bother me. But the inability to communicate is a soul-crushing, spirit-breaking punishment. Not only am I unable to have my needs met, frustrating my caregivers who can't figure out how to help, but this is how I slip into the background and am forgotten in a crowded room. I become no more important than a fixture on the wall or a massive piece of furniture.

Noisy places represent the greatest challenge. If I don't have one of my speech-generating devices cranked up to full volume, any attempt to speak is lost within the din of the surrounding environment. The problem is amplified when I'm talking with someone unaccustomed to interpreting my degraded speech. If asked to repeat myself, I have to expend a considerable amount more effort to be heard and understood. To make matters worse, I have lost control over the muscles in my face, leaving me almost expressionless, which adds an unintended negative quality to my response. Often I must resort to spelling a word letter by letter, those with similar sounds (b/c/d/e/g/v/z, a/j, m/n, q/u, v/z) causing the most confusion.

I needed a way to communicate while I was in bed—or when my eye tracker wasn't working. Fortunately, a clever no-tech solution was developed by Gary Becker, father of the lead guitarist of David Lee Roth's band, Jason Becker. Jason developed ALS in 1996, abruptly ending his stage career. His condition progressed rapidly, and he was only able to move his eyes.

The Vocal Eyes system, requiring two minutes of training, divides the alphabet into six identically sized boxes on a single sheet of paper. One side faces the patient; the other, the caregiver. The patient uses just two movements of either the head or the eyes: the first movement indicates the box and the second movement selects the letter. This tool makes communication possible anytime and anywhere. We use it so frequently that my father created laminated wallet-sized versions and hands them out to everyone we know.

That's the cruel mistress of ALS: I'm fully aware of my environment with all my senses intact, but no ability to call for help when something bothers me.

To get a taste of this, take a few minutes to play along at home on the show *A Day in the Life*.

Sit in a chair and pay particular attention to your surroundings and how your body feels in the space. Mentally scan down—starting with the top of your head and working your way down to your toes. What are the areas of discomfort? Is your shirt not folded quite right against your back? Could your elbow be better positioned on the armrest of the chair? How about the itch that suddenly appeared on your cheek?

Don't move. Don't reposition yourself. Don't scratch that itch.

By now your phone has probably alerted you a few times. Don't answer it, no matter how important you think the message is.

The pterodactyl-sized fly that's been buzzing around all morning decides to perch itself on the ticklish part of your bare foot. Don't shoo it away.

Nose running? Pray you have enough sniffing power to overcome the rate of flow. After all that coffee, your bladder is probably begging for your attention. Or worse, last night's Mexican dinner is starting to make an appearance. Don't get up. And don't call out for help. Remember, you can't.

Welcome to ALS.

Communication is imperative for survival, and alternatives have been developed for nearly every limitation. If you're blind, you can read braille. If you're deaf or unable to speak, you can use written words and sign language. Unable to speak and can't use your hands? You're fucked. I challenge you to get through your day unable to speak, write, or gesture without going batshit crazy.

The eye-tracking solutions, adapted from the user experience design and gaming industries, still have a long way to go before becoming universally accepted as sufficient alternatives to standard communication methods.

• • •

When I first moved in with my parents, they split the caregiving duties. My father, about to retire from his position as director of research at Elan Chemical, handled the night shift. Meanwhile, my mother chose to run her event-planning company, PlanetConnect, from home so she could be available during the day. In no time, they were both worn out, growing older before my eyes. Caring for an adult son isn't the retirement they deserve.

Melissa would help as much as she could on the weekends, but we needed more support. It wasn't long before we started what has been an ongoing hunt for in-home aides to help with the grueling task of caring for me.

There are as many agencies supplying these caregivers as there are patients in need, but it's a challenge finding the right match. My grandmother has had her "girl" for years without so much as a hiccup. Why is my house a revolving door?

Home healthcare is a highly commoditized, high-turnover industry, with a low barrier to entry, like housekeeping. As baby boomers get older and need more care, they are refusing to suffer the same fate as their parents in a nursing home. The desire to age at home is growing along with the demand for aides. The Bureau of Labor and Statistics predicts that the number of jobs will increase by 33 percent through 2030, much faster than the average for all occupations.

At the lowest tier are personal care aides (PCAs), who provide companionship and run errands, collect the mail, and cook on occasion, like the person who helps my grandmother. PCAs are unlicensed, and many states require only a high school diploma.

The National Association for Home Care and Hospice governs the next tier—home health aides (HHAs)—everything from tasks as simple as applying lotion to changing bandages to helping with bathing, dressing, and using the bathroom. This is the kind of help I need. Anything beyond that calls for skilled nursing care, such as a registered nurse.

To earn their HHA certification, applicants must complete seventy-five hours of training, demonstrate their skills, and pass a written examination, though this is the minimum and requirements may be higher in certain states. Having gone through as many HHAs as we have, I can safely say that schooling has zero correlation to the aide's ability to provide care.

I get it, the annual pay is abysmal—$29,430 is the median across the United States—and the aides must tolerate me and the craziness in my house. Why bother getting too invested for fourteen dollars an hour? But ferfuckssake, some of what they're being asked to do is really basic. In fact, they probably do most of the stuff to themselves every day.

As a patient and recipient of HHA services, I'm unwilling to be treated any other way than with dignity and respect. It baffles me why translating my own care and feeding techniques to someone else is so difficult. By the way, HHAs aren't the only caregivers requiring a re-education on this subject. My dear family and friends wishing to lend a generous hand feeding me are just as guilty.

Think about wiping your mouth. Do you wipe from the middle to the outside corners or up and down? Or one big swipe from one side to another? No. Chances are you wipe from one corner to the middle and then the opposite corner to the middle, collecting whatever detritus remains neatly in the middle for removal by either napkin or tongue.

The same goes for cleaning someone's eyes. Always from the inside corner to the outside corner. Never up and down. Try it for yourself. Once you untuck your top eyelashes from your lower lid, I promise you'll understand.

The tedious, time-consuming process of finding help never ends. You call an agency in your area and explain your needs. The Head Nurse in Charge (HNIC) comes to your house, and you explain your needs again, fill out a ream of paperwork, document your needs, and then wait a week or two for the agency to find someone, at which time you schedule a visit. When the new aide and the HNIC come to your house, you explain your needs once more and begin training the new aide. When this aide quits or gets fired, you have to endure this process all over again. I've lost count of how many aides we've been through.

I'm not your average stroke or Parkinson's patient, and I need to be cared for in a particular way. Nothing complex, though seemingly outside the mental capacity of most of these people calling themselves HHAs. The problems we've encountered are pervasive, regardless of the website or agency.

After I lived with my parents for about a year with help from an aide during the morning and my parents taking over the duties from the afternoon through to the next day, they were both burned out, walking around like zombies. I explored the idea of medicating myself with Ambien to help me sleep through the entire night and give them a rest, though apparently sleep aids and classic ALS respiratory issues mix like a long-tailed cat in a room full of rocking chairs.

It was time to get help during the night, so we went back to Caring Senior Services in Essex County, where we'd had success getting matched with our daytime aide, Kemberly. The night shift shouldn't be as demanding as the day shift. No feeding, no pills, and if we set up the last feeding properly, I wouldn't have to get up and pee.

Still, I have sympathy for the caregivers who take on the night shift. How quickly they'll learn that I'm a colossal pain in the ass. Then again, they signed for the gig. Who wouldn't want a night shift advertised as nothing more than helping me pee once a night at most? The rest of the time, they can keep knitting their shark-shaped onesie or catch up on the latest season of *Naked and Afraid*.

If only that were the case.

Sleep for me has become a luxury, with no rhyme or reason as to when I might be graced with its presence.

As my parents and Melissa know, the night starts out easily enough. Step one: Lay me down around 10:30, position the pillows, raise the head of the bed, and stuff my armpits with towels to stop the intense pressure against my sides from my arms contracting involuntarily. Likewise, add hand splints to keep my fingers from contracting.

Now, we're ready for step two, the chemicals: a few puffs on the weed pen to help me off to la-la land and dry the excess saliva. Next, overnight therapeutic (fancy Vaseline) drops in my eyes because they're too weak to stay closed throughout the night, and Chapstick, since I'm apparently a mouth breather now.

Step three: Set the TV to either of my two favorite genres—reality prison and surgery shows or documentaries.

After that, I'm all right on my own while I'm awake watching TV. Once I fall asleep, my body protests with severe ALS-ing, which goes something like this:

I'm uncomfortable. My eyes pop open. *What's bothering me?* My left hand has tightened and is pressing into the mattress. I try to move my hand but can't—too weak. Keep trying. Stress levels rise. *Remember your meditation.* Pulse quickens. Hands sweat profusely. *Screw meditation. I'm not able to fix this on my own. Gotta call for help. I don't hear anyone coming.*

Body temperature skyrockets, legs stiffen into unbendable tree trunks, arms become vice grips against my ribs, hands clench into white knuckle fists. *Where are they?* Call out again. Breathing shallows and panic ensues. Panic! PANIC!

My parents come running, flipping on the lights and attempting to decipher what's causing the stress. Most of the time the panic attacks stem from a feeling of being trapped. Trapped in the bed, trapped in the sheets, even trapped in my own body.

They try desperately to figure out what I need. In the midst of adjusting limbs, towels, and sheets, my legs start shaking violently and breathing requires energy and effort I physically can't expend. *Sit me up! Can't breathe! Sit me up!* My father wraps one arm under my neck, the other under my knees, and, in one swift back-wrenching move, sits me up.

The panic attack stops almost instantly—for a moment. Pop the Xanax and have a few hits of the weed pen, dry the sweat, and try lying down again. Maybe this time I'll sleep. This happens at least eight to ten more times over the next couple of hours, lasting until I pass out, exhausted from struggling to alleviate whatever discomfort my nerves are inflicting on me at the moment.

Needless to say, the bedroom is a major source of anxiety for me.

The process of finding overnight aides is similar to that for daytime aides, only with a drastically smaller pool of candidates. It's a trial by fire. A day of training is typically sufficient, maybe two, if a problem arises.

With each new aide, I go to sleep and see what happens. The usual pattern unfolds—I wake up and need to call for help. *Shit, what's her name? Fuck it, she doesn't know mine, so I'll make any noise I can squeak out and hope she isn't sleeping.* No response. *Didn't she hear me?* Grunt again. My throat hurts now. *Where is she? Come on!* Panic sets in, pulse quickens. I can't hear over the deafening noise of my own heartbeat. Finally the aide appears. As if this were a casual Saturday stroll, she saunters into the room, flips the light on, and hovers over me, waiting for a detailed explanation of the interruption.

The clever aides we've hired point to body parts, thinking they will eventually guess the correct one. Some get there, others keep going over the same parts, hoping I'll change my mind on what is ailing me. After overcoming the communication hurdles, the aide will make the necessary adjustments, and I attempt to sleep once again.

Not unlike the challenges of finding daytime help, many of the night aides have had their own challenges and excuses. Leonard quit because he couldn't handle all the details, which was fine with me since he didn't shower. Raquel quit because she thought she had hurt her back (no lifting was required, by the way), which was code for "I don't want to work this hard." Margaret was fired because she couldn't stay awake.

And then there was Danielle, who was described to us as responsible, dedicated, and caring, the traits of the person you want to take care of your loved ones. Punctual and accompanied by a close personal friend of mine and the owner of the agency, she was ready to start. The thick Haitian accent didn't bother us—after all, it was she who had the difficult task of understanding *me*.

My parents went through the training process, explaining in detail our routine, preferences, and locations of items she would need throughout the night to help me. She nodded at all the appropriate times, indicating that what we were asking her was nothing out of the ordinary.

The smile and nod proved to be misleading. Not until we were in the middle of the night, and she didn't understand why I was protesting her technique for sitting me up, did we realize that the experience she claimed to have was nothing more than hearing about the term ALS.

Danielle never caught on, and we had to fire her.

Please, HHAs, don't assume I'm the same as your previous cases. We're willing to work with any aide, but it's critical to understand the specifics of how I need to be cared for. Ask questions. And for crying out loud, I'm right here in front of you. When you have a question about me, ask me.

The economics of nighttime assistance surprised me. The agency charges the same rate of $25 an hour as the daytime aide but offers a significantly lower work output. Figuring the eight-hour shift is 11:00 p.m. to 7:00 a.m. and I need help ten times throughout any given night for ten minutes each, the agency earns $200 for one hundred minutes of real, actual work that the aide can't seem to manage. That's $200 a night for five nights each week—$1,000 a week and $4,000 a month is exorbitant for the actual amount of work being performed. The daytime aide costs the same but is working constantly.

We explored having a full-time live-in aide but decided against it because that person, tending to me 24/7, would burn out in no time just like my parents.

With intermittent night aides and a consistent daily morning aide, we've averaging between $50,000 and $80,000 a year for HHAs, but the help is worth the expense to give my parents the rest they desperately need. Luckily, I have excellent disability insurance from my employer that covers all the costs.

For those not so lucky, Social Security Disability Insurance (SSDI) provides financial assistance, ranging from $800 to $1,800 a month. Medicare and Medicaid can also help, but they have limitations. HHA services are covered, but only when they are needed to support skilled nursing care, such as assistance with a feeding tube or ventilator.

Even hiring an aide once a week can help ease the heavy burden on family caregivers.

13

Mentor . . . Discover . . . Inspire

AFTER I CAME HOME FROM the Mayo Clinic, my friends and family reached out to me, but I couldn't text more than a few words, let alone see anyone. Todd, the husband of one of my wife's friends, was persistent, acknowledging how overwhelmed I must be. All he wanted, he said, was for me to listen to what he had to say.

Once I was able to pull myself together long enough to have a conversation without falling apart midsentence, I called Todd and told him I was ready.

He got right to the point. "You have lots of women in your life," he said, "but you don't have any strong male support."

That was true. I didn't feel close enough to any of my guy friends to confide in them regularly. But it had never been a problem for me.

Todd went on to tell me about Mentor Discover Inspire—MDI—the men's group he belonged to. "Jeremy, you're going to be facing enormous emotional and physical challenges, and you'll need the type of help only men can give."

What was he talking about?

I was way too deep in my own misery to process or question anything. At that time, I had to immerse myself in constant noise and distractions to keep from breaking down. It was all I could do to get from one minute to the next.

As Todd described the incredible support I would receive from MDI—and how my life was going to change beyond what I was able to imagine—I could barely utter more than a few words of agreement between fits of sobbing. The mute button came in handy.

I took a breath and was about to ask him what the group could possibly do for me when he launched into a deeply personal story, sharing how the men had helped him in his time of need. It was enough to make me sit up and listen.

"Please trust me," he said. "I've told the guys about you so they'll be ready whenever you decide to join us. Give us a chance. You won't regret it."

It took me a month before I dragged myself to the first meeting. Todd had given me the address of a corporate office building near Grand Central that I had passed a hundred times before and told me to be there at 7:30 p.m. sharp. When I arrived, not only were the men expecting me, but one of them had been assigned to help me navigate to the meeting spot on my crutches and make sure I had everything I needed. The welcome wagon they rolled out was certainly impressive.

I can hear what you're thinking: *At the lowest point in your life, Todd shows up and sucks you into a homoerotic,* Eyes Wide Shut*–themed, pseudo-religious cult. Why do you need this group? Men are supposed to be manly. Take off your skirt and don't be a pansy.*

I didn't care. I was willing to try anything that might help.

Just as promised, right when the clock hit 7:30, a man I would later find out was the captain of this team, gruffly announced the time and instructed everyone to form a circle. Rolls were called using only the last names of each man.

The meeting began with different members reciting various

parts of their standards, or code of ethics. The rationale was to create a safe environment that would make everyone feel comfortable sharing deeply personal thoughts, without fear that anything would leave the circle.

Then the captain turned to me. "Schreiber, you're a guest here. Before we proceed, do we have your commitment that you'll keep everything you hear confidential?"

Nodding, I said yes. At that moment, I knew I was with men I could trust.

Each man was given an opportunity to "check in" at a number from one to ten, indicating how he was feeling at the time—the higher the number, the better he felt. I was feeling like shit and checked in at six. Once each man had given their response, those checking in at a six or below were called out to explain. Shit. It would have been helpful to know what was going to happen ahead of time. Too late. "Schreiber, you said you were a six. What's going on that you're not a ten?" the captain asked. "How can we support you to get there?"

One man suggested three options: one, I could simply vent and not receive any feedback; two, I could ask the men for input and guidance; or three, I could ask for something specific. The second option made the most sense.

Eleven complete strangers sat in a circle around me as I shared my story and the reason I had decided to attend the meeting. I hadn't expected how earnestly the men would listen. They weren't simply waiting for the fuckin' new guy to shut up and sit down. I summarized the battle with my health, my fears about what my future would look like, and my angst about the emotional and physical divide at home.

Once I had finished, the men thanked me for having the courage to talk about my feelings with openness and honesty. They asked whether I wanted their input. Yes, I did, very much so, though no way in hell would any of them know what I was experiencing or, for that matter, have anything to say that would be useful. After all, I had lots of friends, albeit predominantly females, so what was the difference between talking with them and what I was doing with these men?

Plenty, it turned out. This wasn't simply shooting the shit with my buddies. These men treated what I shared with the gravity it deserved. They took turns diving into different parts of my story, asking thoughtful questions. It was obvious these men had experienced hardships and triumphs in their lives, and they were able to offer profound insight and support.

I had been to therapy in the past and was in therapy when I attended that meeting. What I received that night benefited me in ways no therapist has come close to achieving.

For the remainder of the meeting, I sat quietly processing what had just occurred. These men had seen me and acknowledged what I was going through with a genuineness few other people in my life could. I needed that support more than I realized.

We continued on for three more hours, following the agenda and time constraints established in the beginning. At the end, the men formed a tight huddle, arms around each other's shoulders. The captain turned to me, since I was the guest, and asked me to summarize what I had learned. I confidently said, "What I learned by being part of this team tonight is that I'm not alone."

Isolation, even when you're surrounded by friends and family, intensifies the feeling of invisibility and is often unavoidable, especially with a rare disease. At the countless walks, conferences, and fundraisers I've attended, I'm one of a small handful of people who is living with the disease. Everyone else is a caregiver, widow, friend, or supporter. It was a sobering experience.

This MDI team, which I later became a member of, affectionately named themselves Massive Dump. When I interact with any of the men in a team setting or one-on-one, I'm treated no differently than any other man. As time has passed and I've had to rely on eye tracking to communicate, they wait a little longer for my response or question, but I'm held to the same standards as everyone else.

The men frequently ask one another how they can support a member in need. When asked, I'm never shy to tell them that human connection is what I need most. If they don't hear from me, they will reach out—to both me and my parents—to let us know we're not alone.

As I've come to discover, the MDI experience has a place in every man's life. Think about that difficult decision you've been putting off. When was the last time one of your friends called you on your bullshit and asked you to commit to making that decision by a certain date and then made you choose your own consequences if you lapsed on that commitment?

Nowhere did that exist in my life except my job. Sure, I was accountable to my wife and had other nonwork obligations, but no one was making sure I actually did the things I knew would help me grow as a man.

The men on my team aren't there to tell me what to do, but rather to support me in the process of becoming the man I always wanted to be. They help me uncover the cause of whatever is holding me back, identify the one or two things I need to do to change my circumstances, and follow up to make sure I take action by the date and time I committed to. If the foundation of MDI was built on anything other than trust and confidentiality, it wouldn't have such a long, successful track record.

Let's use everyone's favorite New Year's resolution as an example—going to the gym. You brag to your buddies that you're going to sweat off the fourth-quarter beer gut and join a gym. Chances are that you're like most of us and have been donating to your gym since last New Year's and haven't stepped foot in there since.

The first of January rolls around yet again. After waking up covered in a thin film of sweat, stale champagne, and shame, you remember your resolution: Go to the gym. But when you arrive, the place is packed. You can smell the booze sweating out of everyone's pores. The whole world seems to have made the same well-intentioned and utterly meaningless resolution. Be honest—you're not going back anytime soon.

When your gym shoes have gone unworn and you have forgotten the combination to your locker, all the well-intentioned momentum for taking care of yourself flies out the window. This is no one's fault but your own. Don't get me wrong, I've been there. But when you feel like shit and your belly button looks like a large cavern in a ball of dough rather than a small cleft in a slab of marble, you have no one to blame but yourself.

Your friends laugh at you because they heard you make these empty promises last year, and the hot receptionist who convinced you to join in the first place has lost interest in your flaccid dad bod.

Every one of us who has had a job has been held accountable—whether to a middle-level manager, shareholders and investors, or to ourselves as the owner of our own company. Why then are we incapable of maintaining that accountability for ourselves when we get home? Why do we allow ourselves to fall short in our personal lives?

This is where your men's team can help. I use "team" and not "group" simply because teams work together toward a common goal. Whether that goal is a service to the community, as in rebuilding part of a man's house destroyed in a flood, or to an individual, as in finding a creative way to help a man meet a health goal, the themes are teamwork, accountability, integrity, and honor.

As part of the learning process in the MDI organization, every member must attend a weekend-long event hosted by the founder, Justin Sterling. My stomach twisted into knots at just the thought of it. I barely had a routine down at home, dressing and feeding myself were becoming more difficult, and frankly, who wants to spend a weekend with a bunch of dudes? It was going to smell like a dirty locker room.

All the men I was getting to know on my team in NYC had nothing but positive things to say about the event and encouraged me to go. After much debate, and in the supportive circle of a weekly meeting, I said "Fuck it" and committed to going, though I knew next to nothing about what I was getting myself into.

I immediately had buyer's remorse.

As the date of the event rapidly approached, I was in full-blown procrastination mode about registering, figuring I could ignore it and not succumb to the influence of the men on my team. It was getting late in the day when I got a call from Max Rosen, one of the more senior members, asking me if he could come over. I knew where this was going, though I highly respected this man and owed him and myself the time to talk through my hesitation.

We sat outside the Dunkin' Donuts on the ground floor of my apartment building for a long time dissecting all my objections. Each one was met with the same two responses: "That's exactly why you need the weekend. Trust the men."

The men? Who were these men and why should I trust them? They didn't know my needs. They didn't know the complexities of caring for me. And why should I ask anyone to be my babysitter? I was dealing with my own mortality and didn't want to waste three days at a conference that wasn't going to benefit my health and well-being in any obvious way.

Ultimately I decided to go.

A man from my team drove me and two other yet-to-be indoctrinated men. We talked and joked nonstop on our way to what was going to become our home for the next two and a half days.

As a fairly seasoned traveler, I've stayed in every type and level of accommodation out there, but believe me when I tell you that past guests were being generous when they gave this murder factory the 1.5 stars on TripAdvisor. Maybe the rooms wouldn't be as bad as the exterior, lobby, hallways, or parking lot. My optimism was getting the better of me.

Two men helped me into my room, and when the door was flung open, I was greeted by an interior decorated by Jeffrey Dahmer and Hannibal Lecter. Maybe it was the carpet being deeply stained with what I hoped was coffee. Or maybe the dark red comforter ready to soak up the day's next kill. Or possibly it was the flickering, incandescent rape light in the bathroom.

When the fear subsided and I was finally able to unclench my asshole, I dropped my bags on the one surface that looked heavily Lysoled and went to the lobby to get this weekend started.

Everyone was milling around talking, and eventually, I needed to use the facilities. At this point I was still using forearm crutches, and aside from these medieval walking sticks being fairly uncomfortable and making me look like Bambi on ice, I was able to walk at a fairly normal pace.

The restrooms were about seventy-five feet away from the lobby. Approaching the men's room door like any nonaccessible door, I leaned a shoulder into it, made a gap, and jammed the foot of the crutch underneath it. This is the time when the kindness of strangers comes in handy, but since I was the only one around, I repeated this shoulder-lean-crutch-plant dance twice more until the opening was wide enough for me to simultaneously slip my body through. I yanked the crutch out from its position as a makeshift door stop before replanting both crutches firmly in front of me, allowing me to take the next step.

The urinals were close to the entrance, and I needed to turn ninety degrees to my right to face one. Still a few feet away, I started my approach. Those crutches and my general difficulty with walking always caused me to spend the majority of the time looking down in front of my feet. As long as the floor appeared stable and clear of debris, it was safe to take the next step.

About a yard from the target, I felt my right crutch begin to slide. No big deal. My legs were stable, and my left crutch was firmly planted, I was certain of it. But as I looked down for obstacles, I realized I was off-balance.

ALS causes the muscles to stiffen, making most movements difficult. Imagine spending all day outside on a frigid winter's day, being inadequately dressed, and coming back inside. How difficult is it to bend your knees? Your arms? Your wrists? Your fingers? That is how my body feels every day. Attempting any quick movements is an exercise in futility. You learn quickly not to bother going after the pen rolling off the table or attempting to hold a closing elevator door.

This stiffness, or spasticity, as the experts call it, prevented me from recovering my stability as I began to fall. I was going down and there was nothing I could do to save myself. While I was falling, I kept thinking, *Please don't land on the piss mat. Please don't land on the piss mat.* Ladies, if you can't envision what I'm talking about, take a quick peek in the men's room one day.

The weekend hadn't officially begun and already I regretted being there. Lying on the cold and slippery floor, I needed help. I felt the warmth of the blood running down the right side of my face, off my chin, and into a small puddle on the floor. I would later come to find out I had whacked my head squarely on the front edge of the urinal. I was forever unclean.

I called out for help five or six times, only the echo of my own voice answering my pleas. No one responded, so I reached for the phone in my pocket, digging with all the strength I had, only to be defeated by my weakened fingers when they loosely folded around the denim that was keeping my phone hostage.

Needing an alternate route to liberate my phone, I slid the rectangular brick to the opening of my pocket from the outside of my pants. Unorthodox, but it worked. Who would I call? The man who drove me that morning had already said goodbye, and the men attending the weekend were all new to MDI, or at least new to me. The only man I could think of to come to the rescue was the man who had brought me into the organization. On the off chance he was in the vicinity, he was my best chance to get help.

I squeezed the sides of my phone to activate Siri, though when I responded, the familiar voice asked me to repeat my command. I was beginning to suffer the speech ailments all too common with ALS. Finally, after repeating the command to place a call, the phone began to dial.

"Help! Are you here? I fell in the bathroom." Was I really about to use this cliché phrase? You better believe I was. "And I can't get up."

At what seemed like lightning speed, four men burst through the bathroom door, picked me up, and slid a chair under me. Conveniently, one of the men was a paramedic, or a doctor, or a random guy who happened to have a roll of gauze on him. They ran through all the standard concussion evaluation questions, but I already knew I was all right. I was more shaken than hurt.

The men lifted the chair bar mitzvah–style and carried me out of the bathroom. Standing in front of us, three other men were rapidly assembling a brand-new push wheelchair for me. Later I found out that this trio had been assigned to look after me all weekend and, in support, took it upon themselves to rush over to the local Walmart and set this up for me. Three complete strangers. A small example of the type of positivity and service that MDI instills in men.

"Chateau Dahmer" provided this solution to the problem: a "Wet Floor" sign in the offending area. No complimentary night stays, no vouchers for the local IHOP (which I'm positive must have been in the area), and no manager in an ill-fitting hand-me-down suit and greasy comb-over groveling for a promise not to sue.

Even so, the feeling of filth, shame, and disgust wore off quickly once the weekend got started. What came next was an unforgettable experience, primarily because of the range of mental, physical, and emotional exercises we endured. Unfortunately, the confidentiality agreement also makes it indescribable.

This wasn't one of those "Tom Cruise jumping on Oprah's couch to convince you he's straight" kind of moments, though after completing the Weekend in May 2018, I can confidently say that it was the best decision I ever made. The only word sufficiently powerful to accurately summarize those two and a half days is "transformative."

If you ask me now what I've gotten out of this organization, I would respond like this:

> Men, I'm Schreiber. For more than three years, I've been battling ALS. You men met me one month after I was diagnosed. My life and my parents' lives have been turned upside down. Physically, I've been imprisoned, and my ability to speak has been robbed. But without this experience and your support, I might never have become the man I wanted to be.
>
> I've broken down barriers once preventing me from owning my truths, from being emotionally open, from strengthening important relationships, and from establishing and upholding my terms. I became determined to begin living with ALS rather than dying from it. Most important, what I learned as a member of Team Massive Dump is that I'm not alone.

Though my tenure as a member of MDI has been relatively short compared to some who clock in at thirty years or more, I've met many men I highly respect. One of those men is Howard Spierer, whom I met at a regional event where teams gathered from all over the tristate region. He was seated in a motorized wheelchair on the covered front porch of the dining hall of the afternoon's rented campground, avoiding the midday sun.

Without a wheelchair of my own, four men carried me in a chair up to the porch to join Howard and three other men who were skipping the latest round of activities. I noticed him first, since he was the only man at this event with a glaringly obvious disability, though my attention quickly shifted to what he was saying, and the disability faded away.

Considered one of the founders of MDI, Howard spoke with purpose and didn't mince words. Any sentiment of a disability was imperceptible, and he wasn't going to be made invisible by anyone who encountered him. Although we have significant differences between our diseases, he became a role model and earned my respect right then and there.

He told me about his experience as a long-term survivor of a chronic and terminal illness:

> I've been at cocktail parties and had to deal with looking at people's backsides. And I've dealt with the frustration of being told that a place is handicapped accessible only to find out that it just has a couple of steps. But generally, I don't feel invisible in my chair, in part because I would tend to be somewhat of an in-your-face kind of guy. I prefer to make it hard for people to ignore me.
>
> That being said, if I have a gripe, it would be about how people tend not to know how to relate to me. I have multiple sclerosis. I've had it for thirty years but have only been without mobility for the last five. Everyone seems to feel that I'm fragile. I certainly don't feel fragile. My version of the disease was a very slow deterioration. For the first twenty years, I was in denial. I was still jumping out of planes, whitewater rafting, basically putting myself at risk.
>
> I think like many people born with disabilities, I worked with what I had, and it didn't feel like I was at a disadvantage. I don't need or want sympathy. I suspect it's different

for people who suddenly find themselves in a new situation. When I started to lose my mobility, I was very conscious of not letting other people perceive that something was wrong. I've come to realize that's more about me than about them.

These days what I want is an opportunity to participate in whatever way possible. It doesn't mean I need to be a part of everything. Sometimes I get equal pleasure just observing others doing something full out. Luckily, before my illness, I had a fairly full life. I have a pretty full memory bank that allows me to enjoy things vicariously because I'm able to remember what it felt like when I did it.

I hate that people stand around and look uncomfortable as they try to figure out how to make me feel included. Any act of participation by me doesn't warrant a massive celebration. Sometimes I try and fail. That's okay. So if you're reading this wondering how you can help, my answer would be to just be yourself and don't worry about my feelings.

14

Be Your Own Healthcare Champion

"You need to be the captain of your healing. You must be vigilant and responsible for your health on every level."
—Dr. Craig Oster

AFTER A DECADE AND A half in sales, I've learned that there is more than one way to get the information you need. This has proven valuable in searching for no-bullshit answers about my condition and new therapies, as well as in rooting out incompetent or shady doctors.

When I developed shin splints after the Brooklyn Half Marathon, I was confident that a few physical therapy appointments would fix me right up and I'd be back running my Central Park loop in no time. Before I could get a prescription for PT, I needed to see a specialist. I could have gone to my primary care doctor, but he would have referred me to a specialist anyway, so I bypassed a step.

Finding an orthopedic doctor isn't easy, at least not in New York, where orthopedic doctors specialize in sections of the body. The foot bone is connected to the leg bone—isn't it that simple? What is the purpose of dividing up the skeleton and allowing only certain surgeons to practice on certain parts?

"It is what it is" is the common response.

I'm willing to bet that this one word is the reason: insurance.

Fine, I'd play along. All I wanted was a script for physical therapy. So I made an appointment with Dr. Carter, an orthopedic surgeon.

When I arrived at his office, the woman at the front desk handed me an electronic tablet and asked me to enter my information. I couldn't help but groan.

Before I continue, I would first like to address certain commonalities (read poor customer service) plaguing outpatient medical offices. These commonalities are learned behaviors by the new office staff from the tenured office staff. Sure, the practice owner could put a stop to the lack of professionalism and compassion, if they weren't seeing ten patients an hour.

An open letter to medical office practice managers:

Dear Practice Managers,

We, as recipients of the care of your practitioners and staff, would like to make you aware of our experience in your offices. We acknowledge that you may not recognize these behaviors, which is why we urge you to pay special attention to the recommendations below.

When you focus first on the satisfaction of the patient, every person involved in the office will benefit.

Before the visit:

Patient portal. Oftentimes, this is the first impression of your practice. It is convenient for patients and the practice alike. For us, it is an easy way to communicate with the office, schedule appointments, and request refills. In your practice, the benefits are measured in hundreds of thousands of dollars in saved man hours. While we understand that the portal is an investment, we will not be responsible for helping you recover your costs.

Paperwork. Request this from the patient *before* the date of the appointment. We do not want to spend a minute longer in your office than we have to. Send us an email with a link to the forms to fill out.

Medications. We will tolerate listing our medications only once. Best practice is to include this request in the paperwork requested before our visit. Once the list is provided, each care provider we interact with during our visit should review this list rather than asking us to list the medications we are taking again. Redundancy for safety is acceptable. Redundancy because you are not paying attention is infuriating. This is a good way to teach your team about communication.

In the waiting room:

Curate your reading material. Ensuring the magazines are current is a baseline responsibility. Have content relevant to your patients. How many people on this planet read *Family Circle*?

Health Insurance Portability and Accountability Act. Comply with it or do not, but choose one. We do not mind coming around the desk to sign in to protect our privacy, as long as you do not then bark out our full name and ailment into the cavernous waiting room for all to hear.

Scheduling challenges, part 1. We are willing to wait up to ten minutes after the start time of our appointment. Any longer and we ask that you proactively notify us with the approximate waiting time. And do not bullshit us. We saw the hot drug rep in the doctor's office waiting to *shtup* him in exchange for writing more of whatever drug she's peddling.

During the visit:

Scheduling challenges, part 2. We understand that your practice cannot buy a single toner cartridge with what our insurance plan reimburses for our visit. But making up for that injustice by cramming in ten patients an hour is inhumane. Do not fight the trend. Let the hospital purchase your practice. Everyone will be better off.

Ancillary services and products. We recognize that practicing medicine is no longer a lucrative profession, and offering cash-paying services like laser hair removal and your own brand of skin care products may be appealing. But we, and probably every medical accreditation organization, suggest you stick with the skills of your specialty. A weekend course on root canals does not turn a dentist into an endodontist.

Eye contact. Our goal in visiting your office is to actually see doctors, not to watch them enter notes into your electronic medical records. Your outcomes will improve when you allow the doctor to focus on us, the patient.

Pro tip. Improve your outcomes to improve your revenue. Before the doctor enters the room, do two things to improve the workflow: Brief the doctor on the reason for our visit and enter our pertinent information in the electronic medical records.

After the visit:

Follow up. The majority of your patients have no medical training, which is why we are in your office. Ninety percent of what we are told is forgotten by the time we get to the parking lot. This means we have to call you to get the same answers we received while we were in your office, creating more work for both of us. At the conclusion of the visit, use that expensive patient portal to send the doctor's notes from the visit. You paid for the feature, so you may as well use it.

We, the patients under the care of your office, acknowledge the complexity of running a medical office. We ask for your consideration in addressing these matters in a timely fashion. This will improve the patients' experience and the workflow of your office.

While we can only call your attention to these issues and ask for your help, please be aware that our ability to wreck your reputation online is far greater than your ability to stop us.

We look forward to continuing our relationship in new and improved ways.

Sincerely,

Committee of Resentful, Angry Patients (CRAP)

The electronic tablet asked for all sorts of information unrelated to the reason for my visit. *Okay, I'll fill out your silly form.* I just wanted to get these shin splints addressed.

A few minutes later, I was ushered in to see Dr. Carter. Nice guy. Professional and caring. He sent me for the requisite "cover your ass by ordering excess tests" X-ray. As compassionate as the doctor was, he had an underlying motive. Not because he was doing something underhanded, but because orthopedic surgeons, no doubt, would rather send patients to the lucrative operating room than prescribe physical therapy.

The next day, the doctor's office called. The X-ray was unremarkable, as I expected, and I was given the green light to begin physical therapy.

When I arrived for my first appointment, I was greeted by Dr. Wilson, the owner and operator of the facility. He reviewed the reason for my visit and then proudly highlighted the other services he offered, so much so that I'd almost forgotten why I was there. Finally, he introduced me to John, the therapist, and we could get started.

After the first few sessions, Dr. Wilson approached me, inquiring about my experience at the practice so far. In the same breath, he recommended I allow him to check for potential misalignment of my spine and hips. When I told him my insurance didn't cover chiropractic, he waved his hand dismissively. "If your insurance doesn't cover it, don't worry about it."

What did that mean? I didn't ask, but I knew I'd remember his offer if the time ever came.

He had a high-volume practice, one physical therapist working on multiple patients simultaneously. The gold standard is one-on-one care. In the same room, across from the four PT tables, was a regularly scheduled Pilates class run by Florence, the angriest French woman I had ever met. Maybe she wasn't angry—perhaps she was simply reviewing her grocery list. I couldn't tell one way or the other. *C'est la vie!*

Large exercise equipment took up the remaining quarter of the cramped room. Space is understandably at a premium in Manhattan, but this was excessive.

Wilson frequently stopped by during my PT sessions and asked how I was feeling, directing me to the chiropractic table when I was done. Great customer service! Or so I thought. A pattern began to develop in his seemingly altruistic drop-by. Wilson would appear only when Florence was teaching her Pilates classes. Aha! So he was a smooth talker and a dirty old man.

Weeks turned into months as I diligently attended the twice-weekly PT sessions. My shin splints had only marginally improved, and I began noticing that my right leg seemed weaker than my left. John, my physical therapist extraordinaire, focused the sessions on rebuilding the strength in that leg.

Somewhere around that time, I reviewed my insurance EOBs—explanation of benefits—and saw a few additional charge codes from that office. I called the billing number and asked to speak with the person handling Dr. Wilson's patients. "Oh, she's at lunch," was the reply. Next time, I was told, "She's not available," and later in the week, "She's on vacation." Someone didn't want me asking questions.

I took the paperwork with me to the next PT session. After exchanging pleasantries with the receptionist, I showed her the extra codes and played dumb. "I get these forms all the time, but I hardly ever look at them. Can you tell me what these numbers mean?" This wasn't my first EOB rodeo, and something wasn't right.

The receptionist attempted to reconcile the insurance statements against my chart on her computer. Walking down the list, she told me which dates I had been treated by Wilson or another practitioner in the office.

"No. Nope. Wasn't here then. Don't know who that is."

She quickly became flustered and asked me to speak with Wilson in his office.

The doctor invited me in and asked me what he could help me with. I pointed to the extra charges and said that the receptionist and I couldn't make heads or tails of them or of the three additional codes tacked onto each date of service.

"We automatically add those codes for our patients," he said. "You can just ignore them."

"Can you tell me what they're for? I know one of them is for PT, but what about the others?"

He looked at the charges and said nothing.

"My insurance was billed on all of these dates with the extra codes. Was it an error? If it was, no problem, I'll give my insurance company a call and explain."

"How much?" he asked.

"How much what?" I wanted to see how far down the rabbit hole I could take this.

"Tally up the amount you were overcharged, and I'll cut you a check."

Considering it was the insurance company he was attempting to defraud, I couldn't figure out why he wanted to cut me a check. If I weren't so deathly afraid of karma, I would have taken the money, and *then* called the insurance company. But I was about to finish the PT sessions in another week and didn't want to entangle myself any further, so I said I'd let him know.

Fuck that! I told John what happened, and I was outta there.

Once I got back to my apartment, I did a little digging through all my EOBs generated by Dr. Wilson's office and found that this had been going on since my first visit. I called the fraud department of my insurance company and recommended they do some digging of their own.

I get it—medicine doesn't pay what it once did, and you need to find creative ways to improve your revenue. But, dude! C'mon. If you're gonna scam insurance companies, be discreet. A little bit here, a little bit there, and chances are no one will notice. Like that old saying "Pigs get fat, hogs get slaughtered."

A few weeks later, I decided to google the good doctor just for shits and giggles. Turns out he was more than a dirty old man scamming insurance companies. Appears he was a bit of a woman hater. When Wilson interviewed potential new female employees, he asked about their reproductive plans. If the candidate hinted at being even the slightest bit interested in getting pregnant, Wilson would immediately dissuade her from pursuing the job. And what if you were caught being pregnant on the job? Adios! Wilson would unceremoniously show you the door, just as he did with the three women who brought a lawsuit against him.

It's important to know there are specific laws protecting against pregnancy discrimination. Wait. What am I talking about? We shouldn't need laws for this because no one should be that bad at being human.

Apparently, these laws exist for people like Dr. Wilson.

So several million dollars in damages later, it's no longer a mystery why he decided to start scamming insurance.

15

Why Can't I Get an Answer?

THE EXHAUSTIVE EFFORTS MY FAMILY and I put into finding out what was wrong with me are not uncommon. On average, it takes one year for a person to get a definitive diagnosis of ALS. For me, it was closer to a year and a half. Why does it take long?

As many as 30,000 people in the United States are living with ALS. Some 90 percent of the cases are considered sporadic, meaning there's no known cause. If you served in the military, you're twice as likely to get ALS, no matter what branch you served in or where you were deployed. The remaining 10 percent of cases are familial. If your father or mother passed away from ALS, unless it was sporadic, there's a 50 percent chance you're next.

In the United States, there are about 17,000 board-certified neurologists. Over the life of their practice, they may see only a small handful of ALS patients, so their experience is limited. At the current time, no single test exists to identify sporadic cases. Compounding the diagnostic process are the many diseases and conditions that can mimic ALS, like Lyme disease, myasthenia gravis, and heavy metal intoxication, to name a few.

And ALS is not one disease. As we have come to use the word

"cancer" as a layperson's catchall phrase, we know dozens of types of cancer exist, and even more ways to get it. We also understand there's no singular treatment for all types.

Not long ago, HIV and breast cancer were death sentences. It's only a matter of time before the types, origins, and treatments of ALS are identified.

By the spring of 2017, I knew the weakness in my leg wasn't structural and started looking for a neurologist near my apartment, just to rule out anything serious. Dr. Andreas Neophytides, New York University Hospital, did what I would later learn was a typical neurological examination. To assist him in making a diagnosis, he sent me to get an MRI (magnetic resonance imaging) scan of my brain and entire spine, called the cervical, thoracic, and lumbar (CTL) regions. The report would tell him whether any lesions were present, indicating the possibility of multiple sclerosis (MS).

When I returned to his office for the results, Dr. Neophytides told me the scan was unremarkable. "This is one of three things," he said. "A pinched nerve, multifocal motor neuropathy (MMN), or motor neuron disease (MND). Unfortunately, this is out of my expertise."

He referred me to Dr. Hiroshi Mitsumoto at Columbia Presbyterian Hospital. Well-published, Dr. Mitsumoto was working on leading-edge research in neurology, and more specifically MNDs.

In the four weeks I waited to see the doctor, I went to a spinal surgeon to rule out the pinched nerve issue. Armed with the growing folder of my records, I shared the report and DVD of the head and CTL scan. Again, unremarkable. So no pinched nerve or slipped disc.

It was a hike and a half to Dr. Mitsumoto's office on 168th Street and Fort Washington Avenue. After a solid hour on the subway, I landed right in front of his office. A man of few words, he ordered more tests, including blood work and what would become the first of many electromyography tests. An EMG measures muscle response or electrical activity in response to a nerve's stimulation of the muscle and is used to help detect neuromuscular abnormalities. During the test, small electrodes (like needles) are inserted into the muscle. Every muscle. Repeatedly. And then wiggled around. Repeatedly.

Another two weeks and I was back in Dr. Mitsumoto's office to discuss the results. He told me that whatever was happening to me was due to my nerves demyelinating. He quickly sketched the problem on a scrap of paper and talked me through what was happening. The myelin sheath protects the nerves and allows electrical impulses to transmit efficiently along the nerve cells. Some diseases damage the sheath and can cause problems in the brain, the eyes, the spinal cord, and other parts of the body.

He agreed with Dr. Neophytides: whatever I had was either MMN or MND. The next step: intravenous immunoglobulin (IVIg) infusions, an aggressive and expensive therapy to be administered over the course of six hours, twice a week, for the next three months. My body's response to the treatment would help him determine which condition I had.

I started asking a slew of questions, mostly aimed at trying to get Dr. Mitsumoto to admit that it wasn't a big deal, just take two of these and call him in the morning. No go. The doctor needed to move on to another patient. He was all business and a bit blunt, but I didn't care. He could have thrown his coffee at me as long as he could help me.

I still worked at the time and was able to set up the infusions at home rather than at the typical infusion center. Sitting in a hospital version of a living room recliner twelve hours a week, next to six to eight other people each getting their own infusions, wasn't my idea of fun.

Week after week for three months, the nurse came to our tiny apartment and administered bag after bag of immunoglobulin. I did my best to stay off Google—I was scared enough already. I poured all my energy into my job, doing as much as I could from my apartment and avoiding face-to-face customer meetings whenever possible.

Not wanting to return to the Upper, Upper, Upper West Side to be hurried along by Dr. Mitsumoto, I searched for a highly regarded neurologist with a deep interest in research. Basically, I wanted an equivalent to Dr. Mitsumoto, but closer to my apartment.

In August 2017, all my research led me to Dr. Dale Lange. A rock star. Chairman of neurology and neurologist-in-chief at the Hospital for Special Surgery and a professor of neurology at Weill Medical College of Cornell University. He's an attending physician at both the Hospital for Special Surgery and New York Presbyterian Hospital's Weill Cornell campus—and also the current president of the New York State Neurological Society.

Whatever all that meant, I knew this was the guy. I had to get on his calendar. But his website said he wasn't taking any new patients. Fuck.

A career in sales had taught me that "no" is relatively meaningless. I built a packet of all things relevant to my case, and along with a handwritten letter (yes, seriously), I went to his office and waited. Not wanting to hand my survival over to a disgruntled desk jockey in his waiting room, I asked for the highest level clinical and research manager on his staff. Mona greeted me in the lobby.

I explained my purpose for coming in person and that I understood the practice wasn't accepting new patients. I asked if she would personally hand the packet to Dr. Lange, and she agreed.

Next step: I found Dr. Lange's personal email address and wrote the same letter I had handwritten. If that didn't work, I wasn't above figuring out how to make my way into his kitchen and waiting there. I'm kidding . . . sorta.

Just a few days later, Dr. Lange's office called and said he would take me on as a patient, quickly scheduling an appointment for me. How was that? Remember, I hand delivered all the pertinent information about my case to him. That way, I eliminated any precursor tests, potentially delaying an initial visit.

First things first. A new doctor meant new tests. I got it—the MRI, EMG, and blood work I received last week on the west side of town couldn't possibly match up to the MRI, EMG, and blood work on the east side of town. I was beginning to feel like a human pin cushion.

Dr. Lange ordered additional tests, including full genetic sequencing, a diffusion tensor image of my brain (done in an MRI to look for iron deposits), and a magnetic stimulation test (approved for treating depression and migraines but also used for nerve conduction studies).

He had a kinder manner and was willing to take as much time answering questions as I needed. His approach to my case was different than any other practitioner I had encountered in my personal or professional experience. He was attempting to build a case for a nondestructive disease. The flu isn't destructive. Hell, most cancers and even HIV had become walks in the park. Whatever I had was doing some awful things to me.

While I was being poked and prodded from all angles, I had plenty of time to think. Aside from the immediate concern of *This nurse gets only one more chance to find my vein,* the thought that kept bouncing off the front of my brain was *If this is what I'm left with, I can handle it.*

Dr. Lange kept me on the IVIg infusions for a few more months, eventually making the diagnosis of stiff-person syndrome. Feel free to snicker like a fifth-grade delinquent in wintertime who poured water on the stairs and is waiting for his math teacher to tumble down the icy concrete steps. But this disease was far rarer. Like one-in-a-million rare. Go big or go home?

After a few weeks of adjusting to the idea of that diagnosis, I still had questions. I was already on the one treatment for this rare disease—the IVIg infusions—but I wasn't improving. And I had symptoms that didn't fit in with any of the four types.

Back to square one.

16

My Own Personal Quarterback

AS I STARTED GOING TO more and more doctors, I discovered that they were hyper-specialized in their training but didn't have even a cursory understanding of different and possibly beneficial alternative therapies available in their own field of study. Add this to all the research I was doing on my own about experimental therapies, and I needed a quarterback to help straighten this all out.

My employer at the time, Perfecto Mobile (now called Perforce), approached me asking how they could help. We tossed around a few ideas, mostly focused on the company paying for one or two large expenses. Unfortunately, I wasn't at the stage where I knew what needed to happen to get better.

The chief revenue officer called to tell me his wife had a suggestion that he thought I would like. She knew a woman named Barbara, a nurse by training who had become a healthcare advocate. I had never heard of this, but the concept made perfect sense. She could be the quarterback I was looking for.

Throughout most of my professional working career, I worked for massive global companies—Sanofi Aventis, GE Healthcare, and Oracle—companies so large that being considered a cog in the machine would have been a promotion. If I had gotten sick while working for one of those behemoths, I'm sure the line item I represented would have been replaced by an equally insignificant line item—at half the cost.

I was fortunate to have worked for Perfecto. The founder and executive team built a family-first culture that I was proud to call myself a part of.

After speaking to her only once on the phone, quarterback Barbara asked me to meet with her at her apartment. Sixty-something, eclectic, pops of purple in her jet-black hair, she lived in one of the last rent-stabilized, nonaccessible apartments in NYC. We talked for almost two hours, reviewing what had occurred over the past year. She committed to building a plan for me that would incorporate a multitude of therapies she was certain would be worth trying. Sounded good to me.

In no time, Barbara assembled a team of three holistic medical doctors, each with a different approach to medicine. Against my better judgment, my father's continual protesting, and a lack of real clinical evidence to support the majority of the holistic and homeopathic techniques, I was willing to try anything.

One of the doctors assembled an orangey-color concoction of different orthomolecular powders I had to get down my throat twice a day. Another doctor gave me reiki treatments once a week. And the third administered "upbuilding and neuroprotective" infusions. This was in addition to the twice-weekly IVIg infusions, my job, and my ongoing search for more answers.

Nearly four months of getting bombarded by this regimen failed to yield any changes, positive or negative. When I asked Barbara to bring the team together for a review of my case, they presented the golden trifecta of rationale:

1. The treatment works, which is the reason your disease has stabilized.

2. The treatment works, but you're not a responder to the treatment, and your disease is stable regardless of the treatment.
3. The treatment didn't work, and your disease is stable for some other reason.

Rarely does a patient hear the third reason. That would be an admission that the doctors were punching above their weight. In other words, they didn't have a fuckin' clue how to help me.

Neither my time nor money was wasted by this process. When you deal with an unknown medical issue, it's important to stay open to all types of options. I looked at it as a fact-finding mission, and Barbara was instrumental in helping me.

Searching for expertise became my full-time job. Anyone with an internet connection can put up a "Top Ten Best Doctors" list and waste an ungodly amount of your time with legitimate-looking articles that turn out to be well-crafted click bait for Russian brides and hair restoration clinics. I went a different route, searching instead for volume of clinical publications, endowments, and any general online activity in neurological disorders. This weeded out the chaff. High activity equals big budgets.

The Mayo Clinic was a consistent front runner. Among the four campuses to choose from, it made sense to visit their headquarters in Rochester, Minnesota, where the most neurological work was done. Coincidentally, that campus offered a second opinion program—over the course of five days, a team of specialists would run a patient through a battery of tests and provide a definitive diagnosis. Exactly what I was looking for.

I reached out to the program coordinator to get all the details. Once I had sent all my records and they reviewed them, they would let me know whether I had been approved for the program. If I was,

I would receive a few appointment dates. Two weeks later, they called to tell I was accepted, and I chose the first available date—New Year's Day, 2018.

That meant taking a trip to Minnesota . . . in January . . . in the winter . . . when it's fifteen degrees below and snowing. None of that mattered. To get an answer, I would travel through blizzards while fighting polar bears.

All I had to do was book the flights for my parents and myself, since Mayo would take care of scheduling everything else, including all the tests, the hotel, and transportation to and from the airport. I had just finished my most successful year at work, earning a spot in the prestigious President's Club, so the first week of January was the perfect time to take off for a week and get this taken care of.

I still hadn't told my company about the seriousness of my condition. It was mostly because I was in denial myself.

As we prepared for the trip, it dawned on me to triple-check the flights. *Fuckitty fuck!* Who knew there was more than one Rochester? The Delta agent was super sympathetic and changed our tickets to the correct Rochester. Oops.

The weather was just as brutal as expected—it was a whopping two below zero when we landed. What a relief to discover that the clinic had a network of underground tunnels linking the hospital to many of the surrounding buildings.

The packet of instructions I received before we left made for a smooth process when we got there. The Mayo Clinic app would provide the latest schedule, test results, and a way to communicate with my clinical team. *This* is the way every healthcare facility should operate.

Our quarterback for the week was Dr. Andrew McKeon. He walked us through the agenda, answering many of our questions before we had a chance to ask.

Starting that same afternoon, the tests were nearly identical to those I had done over the last few months. MRI, EMG, spinal tap (also known as lumbar puncture, or LP), and over forty vials of blood. The phlebotomists were dead-on with the cannula every time, making the repeated jabs slightly more tolerable. Only one didn't get my joke when I asked when the blood would be returned to me. Admittedly a poor attempt at cracking a joke, but humor was the only way we were going to make it through the week without breaking down each time we thought about the worst-case scenario.

I would eventually become a pro at LPs, receiving my eleventh in early 2020. But the one at the Mayo Clinic was only my second, and the throbbing headache afterward was like nothing I had ever experienced. About half the people undergoing the procedure will get this vicious side effect. To prevent it, the patient needs to lie flat for an hour and guzzle caffeine. Neither helped. We told Dr. McKeon, and less than twenty minutes later, I was facedown on an operating table receiving a "blood patch."

The mechanics of the headache are straightforward. Our brains float in this sticky fluid called cerebrospinal fluid. The LP removes some of that fluid, causing the brain to sit lower in the head. Our bodies don't like changes and use pain to signal that something is wrong. At this point, my brain was screaming at me. The blood patch is a clever technique to physically lift the brain in the skull. Half an hour later, the pain was gone!

As the test results came trickling in one by one, we attempted to interpret them and make our own case for why all this had a simple explanation that could be easily solved by taking just one little pill.

The days flew by, packed with test after test. Dr. McKeon, as part of the program, asked us to have his colleague Dr. Elie Naddaf examine me. Both were neurologists, but Dr. Naddaf's focus was on autoimmune-related neurological disorders. He wasn't convinced that I had run-of-the mill MMN or MND. Instead, he thought it was something autoimmune-related, which made sense because he was looking through autoimmune-colored glasses.

Finally, it was time to meet with our quarterback for the final verdict. Over the next thirty minutes, Dr. McKeon explained his methodology for reaching the ALS diagnosis and what it meant for me and for us.

We sat in the lobby for hours, taking turns crying, but the only thing left to do was to go home and reinvent our lives.

I continued to see Dr. Lange as my primary neurologist. Based on the diagnosis from the Mayo Clinic, he stopped the IVIg infusions and switched over to the two ALS medications—Riluzole and Nuedexta. Neither drug would probably have much effect, but they weren't a big deal to swallow, so I continued taking them.

Even though the diagnosis was the worst possible scenario, it gave me a starting point to begin researching potential therapies and clinical trials.

News about Brainstorm Cell Therapeutics' Phase 3 trial of their product NurOwn was everywhere. This treatment uses stem cells from a patient's own bone marrow and matures them into cells that produce high levels of neurotrophic factors, molecules that promote nerve cell growth and survival. These cells are then injected into the patient's spinal canal to encourage nerve cell repair, with the goal of slowing the disease.

Getting admitted to this trial became my primary focus. With 20,000 applicants around the world, and only 300 spots, I needed to make a strong case or be professionally persistent (a huge pain in the ass). It was a combination of both that eventually got me a golden ticket.

Beginning in August 2018, and for the next eleven months, my parents and I would make the two-hundred-plus-mile trip from New Jersey to the University of Massachusetts Medical School in

Worcester fourteen times. Nearly half the trips consisted of thirty-minute "progress evaluations": the team would take my vitals and run them through the standard Amyotrophic Lateral Sclerosis Functional Rating Scale-Revised to measure my rate of decline. Oh yeah, and they collected a urine sample. I so badly wanted to bring a sample from one of my pregnant friends, just to make the trip more exciting.

The team was spearheaded by lead site investigator Robert Brown, MD, famous for his discovery of the SOD-1 gene mutation associated with causing the familial type of ALS. He was joined by a top-notch osteopathic physician, neurology research nurse, and research project director. An all-star cast.

Having this kind of access to world-renowned researchers wasn't lost on us. We took every opportunity to ask questions about ALS, though due to the double-blind nature of this trial, the team was able to answer only certain ones.

I had just started this journey, but I was getting closer to finding credible, reliable resources that would make a difference in the quality and longevity of my life. Sadly, I would come to learn that I had received the placebo during the trial.

Was it worth the year of effort? Yes. I had a 50 percent chance of receiving the real drug, which is infinitely greater than if I hadn't participated. And the ALS research community learned something. At the time of writing, NurOwn appears to be the greatest hope to finally ending ALS.

(*Publisher's note*: The trial results show that NurOwn may provide meaningful clinical benefit for ALS patients with less advanced disease.)

17

Never Give Up

"In life, winning and losing will both happen.
What is never acceptable is quitting."
—Earvin "Magic" Johnson

AFTER I MOVED BACK TO New Jersey, it wasn't practical to keep humping back and forth to the upper east side of NYC to see Dr. Lange. I needed an ALS clinic nearby that had the coordinated support of the specialties required to care for the disease. Out of the three clinics in the state, Robert Wood Johnson University Hospital at Rutgers University in New Brunswick is the closest. It doesn't hurt that Evelyn's, our favorite Lebanese restaurant, is there.

Who gets to be my Doctor o' the Week this time, Johnny? (Drum roll, please . . .)

In the fall of 2018, Dr. Megan Leitch took center stage.

Lasting four to five hours every three months, ALS clinic appointments are marathons of getting poked and prodded. I'm shuffled from the neurologist to the social worker to get weighed (not an easy task), to the nutritionist, to the speech pathologist, to the respiratory therapist, to the occupational therapist, and finally to the physical therapist. Oh yeah, and they want the requisite sample. A great group of clinicians. Compassionate, encouraging, and resourceful.

Because of the gravity of this disease, I have an extreme sense of urgency to get answers. Dr. Leitch tends to be conservative in that regard. News about novel treatments and clinical trials arrive in my inbox daily, and I need feedback from someone on the bleeding edge of all things ALS. Melissa is my go-to for this. She has been instrumental in finding the right treatments no matter where in the world they may be.

Belief in Western, so-called modern medicine leaves me with lots of unanswered questions. Without getting wrapped around the axle on how the FDA chokes innovation or how clinical studies in the ALS disease state are poorly designed, making them largely inaccessible to most patients, the treatment options available here in the United States are limited. While the ALS community waits for treatment breakthroughs to hit the market, people who have the disease are forced to look at alternative and off-label therapies (AOTs).

Dr. Richard Bedlack, an ALS researcher at Duke University, created ALSUntangled, a database of AOTs derived from patient demand. Dr. Bedlack and an internationally dispersed team of researchers evaluate the AOTs with the greatest number of votes. The results are given a grade across five categories: mechanism, preclinical, cases, trials, and risks. This database has been one of our top resources whenever a potential therapy hits our radar.

The summer before, in June 2019, we had the opportunity to meet Dr. Bedlack and hear him speak at the ALS Advocacy Conference in Washington, DC. Reminiscent of the famed Patch Adams, MD, Dr. Bedlack dressed in the most bizarre outfits, explaining that it was a way to bring joy to his office and the patients he cared for. Brilliant as he was fascinating, he spoke about his approach to finding a cure for ALS and his philosophy when treating patients. To say this doctor was an out-of-the-box thinker didn't do him justice. For Dr. Bedlack, there was no box.

Over the next several months, I emailed Dr. Bedlack with the occasional question. Even though I wasn't his patient, he always replied within a few hours. It became evident that he and his team needed to see me sooner rather than later, but I had to wait two months for an appointment. We scheduled it in March 2020.

His clinic is located at Duke University in Raleigh, North Carolina. Oh, happy days! We would have to take another fun-filled family trip in the van.

Anytime I travel now, it's a monumental effort for everyone involved. So much so, in fact, that we created an "ING" list, as in traveling, shopping, packing, to ensure nothing gets left behind. Many simple items are easy to forget if you don't use them every day, like sunscreen, passport, or electrical power converters. All hell would break loose if the portable bidet or my pills were left behind—and for that matter, any weed paraphernalia. My parents have taken the list to such granularity that "suitcase" is on it. Looking more closely at it, I'm sure I would find my name on there as well.

As we prepared for our trip to North Carolina, I had flashbacks of every family drive the Schreibers have taken since I started using the power wheelchair. It goes something like this:

- T minus two days: My father's nerves kick into overdrive. The ING list is discussed, printed, revised, and then printed again. The weather forecast is announced and repeated every hour.
- T minus one day: The van is filled with gas. The ING list is reviewed and amended by hand. The weather is also reviewed, reinterpreted, and disagreed with based on the intensity of my father's headache. I introduce the idea of taking a few puffs of the vape to address the stress levels.
- T minus six hours: Someone is about to be declared an asshole. Not one of the three of us, but someone who may or

may not be involved in this excursion. This is inevitable, a moment when the "duck and cover" safety technique must be deployed.

- T minus four hours: We're now no longer in control. Fiber has stepped in and grabbed the reins due to my parents' obsession with healthy colon activity. Surely the pot of high-test caffeinated coffee had nothing to contribute to this craptastic cacophony synchronized with the William Tell Overture.
- T minus two hours: An item requiring easy access during the trip fails to make itself obvious and easily accessible. My mother begins to clean. My father locks and loads the fanny pack, once said item is placed within reach, into the van.
- T minus one hour: Something without relevance to the trip becomes front and center priority numero uno. The lower our ability to exert influence over whatever has just arisen, the greater the attention it will require at this very moment.
- T minus forty-five minutes: I step onto the stage, the spotlight focuses on me, and the crowd goes quiet. Whatever hasn't been done to me yet to get me out of the door is about to happen with the fervor of a mother bear rushing her cubs out of harm's way. Shoes? Check. Teeth brushed? Check. Now is the opportunity to take a piss or risk waiting until we find a roadside rest stop that doesn't bear obvious signs of drug deals gone bad.
- T minus fifteen minutes: Shuffle everyone and everything into the van. Four bags, three people, one super-heavy motorized wheelchair. Then two more trips to the bathroom.
- T minus five minutes: Houston, we have a problem. Something isn't right. Quick, go check the oven, I think I left it on. No. Wait. It's off. I hear something running in the house. Aha! The goddamn toilet is flushing on its own. Why? Why wouldn't it? Strap the wheelchair down, adjust all mirrors,

ensure a sufficient supply of tissues are at the ready, windows wide open, and "Is everyone buckled in?"

- T minus zero . . . lift off! Finally backing out of the driveway. At this point, everyone is swearing like Clark Griswold in *National Lampoon's Christmas Vacation.*

But it doesn't get any better. What follows is a stressful drive, mostly because of the van itself, a heavily modified 2016 Dodge Grand Caravan. We raised the height of the van, lowered the floor, and installed a ramp through the side door. The middle-row seats and front-passenger seat were removed to allow me to drive my wheelchair in, do a K-turn, and secure the chair in a lock installed on the floor. These added complexities made the Scooby mobile heavier, less aerodynamic, noisy, and uncomfortable.

I have no choice but to ride shotgun, aware of that position's considerable responsibility. The front passenger must be alert for the entire trip, make the driver aware of traffic dangers and fast-lane opportunities, manage the GPS mapping software and upcoming directional changes, identify gas price options while selecting the least expensive, and, probably the most important, be the DJ. For any able-bodied passenger, this requires intense concentration, good dexterity, and a steady supply of caffeine. In my current state, none of the above describes me.

Early on, after I sat down in the wheelchair, I would make the final adjustments and be ready to go. Similar to lying down to sleep, once you have positioned yourself in the perfect spot in bed, you don't want to move. But now, this beast of a disease causes incredible stiffness of all my muscles, making quick and responsive movements impossible.

Whenever the wheelchair goes over a bump, whether I'm in the car or outside, my limbs stiffen up, my feet begin to shake, and my hand pops off the joystick. This happens with every bump. If we include the rest of my symptoms—watering eyes, incessant and intolerable yawning, and inability to speak—I'm officially the worst candidate for copilot on any excursion. I neglected to mention that my father is deaf in one ear and my mother is losing her hearing in both. Not that it would be easy for anyone in the third row of seats, where my mother sits, to hear the driver and passenger speaking.

Adding music to the journey should calm the nerves, except it does the opposite. Since the five-year-old stock radio seems overly complex, I plug in my phone and set up Spotify for music and Waze for directions to play through the van's radio. If you're familiar with either of these apps, you'll agree there are certain known knowns. Spotify, for example, plays a list of songs and then stops or starts over. Waze is never to be challenged. Choose an alternate option at your own peril.

On all our drives together, I set up these two apps, though without fail, both my parents react as though they've never seen them before. The same could be said about the temperature controls in the van, the Apple TV remote, and anything having to do with answering or hanging up a call on a cell phone.

As if ALS weren't difficult enough, my appointment with Dr. Bedlack coincided with the arrival of the coronavirus, which grabbed the world's population by the short and curlies and rapidly tightened. Since we would be traveling two days each direction, we needed assurances that they would see me if we made the trip.

Every time we called Bedlack's office, the restrictions on social distancing and self-isolation became ever more restrictive. I could still be seen, they said, but the number of people allowed to accompany me had decreased from two to one. This meant someone was sitting in the car for the duration of the visit. *Congrats, Dad, you have been volunteered.*

As I do with all the clinicians I engage with, I emailed details of my current medications and list of questions in advance, and these were sitting on top of Dr. Bedlack's stack of papers when my mother and I walked into his office.

After a more thorough neurological examination than I'd had in the past, he answered each of our questions one by one. All the hassles of traveling down there were worth it.

Dr. Bedlack, having personally verified over forty ALS reversals (meaning the patient had a confirmed case of ALS before returning to a pre-ALS baseline), said he wasn't going to assume that I had ALS. He needed to confirm it himself with additional tests that I hadn't previously had.

With a deep understanding of the standards of care treatments and alternative therapies, he made multiple changes to my self-directed protocol of pills and potions. In some cases, he was forthright: "We studied that, and it didn't work. Here's the paper we wrote on it."

Although my breathing had been measured at other clinics, recently showing a steady decline, Dr. Bedlack was the only one to give it to me straight—I needed to decide within the next three to four months whether I wanted to get a tracheostomy. (An opening created in the front of the neck so a tube can be inserted into the windpipe to help with breathing.)

Six hours later, we emerged from Dr. Bedlack's clinic and headed back to the hotel. I would continue to see Dr. Leitch at her clinic, with input from Dr. Bedlack via telemedicine. It turned out that I was the last patient he saw before the hospital closed its doors due to the coronavirus outbreak.

Finding the answers to complex questions isn't easy. It takes a positive mental attitude, an insatiable appetite for chasing leads, and a team that supports you unconditionally. I'm blessed to have all three and couldn't imagine where I would be without them.

18

Always Start at the Top

"If I am not for myself, who will be for me? If I am only for myself, what am I? And if not now, when?"
—Rabbi Hillel

AS A MEMBER OF THE ALS ASSOCIATION, I had the opportunity to go to Washington, DC, to meet with senators and congressmen to influence their vote on issues pertaining to the disease.

I didn't have a clue how the government really worked. I knew it was my duty to vote, and I did so faithfully. Because the electoral college is in place and I live in a traditionally blue state, my individual vote doesn't have much impact.

When the 2016 election rolled around between Hillary Clinton and that burning dumpster fire Donald J. Trump, I watched as a slow-moving train wreck careened off the tracks, sliding straight up America's ass. It cemented my disgust at the entire political process.

This opportunity in DC was profoundly different. It was a guaranteed way I wouldn't be invisible, and I would also be able to make my voice heard directly by the people who could have an impact—my senators from New Jersey and the representative from my district.

• • •

In June 2019, my parents and I joined the National ALS Association of seven hundred ALS patients, caregivers, and advocates in Washington, DC, for the annual ALS Advocacy Day. We had a lot of work ahead of us: two days of preparation followed by a day of back-to-back meetings with these members of Congress and the Senate.

Rather than enduring five hours each way of tense driving in the Scooby mobile, I pushed my parents into accepting the convenience and speed of the train. What a relief.

Given that the ALS Association set up the conference, they were keen to choose hotels with ADA-compliant rooms. But I wasn't surprised to find that our hotel room at the Washington Marriott Metro Center, much like most other so-called ADA-compliant environments, was unusable.

A standard height toilet, a normal bathtub (which I was unable to access), a bathroom sink with no room for my knees, and the most bizarre of all: thirty-six-inch-high beds, which were comically difficult to get into. Mr. Marriott, you have missed the mark in a bad way. Fuck it. We aren't here to lounge around, are we? No! We're here to change the world!

The agenda wasn't for the faint of heart. All seven hundred of us rolled, walked, and shuffled into the JW Marriott's massive ballroom, sitting with each of our respective regions. The Greater New York region was almost thirty-strong. I had formed relationships online with many of them in ALS support groups and was now able to meet them in person. It was gratifying to make new friends who understood what I was going through and who saw me. Really saw me.

With all of society's efforts to ignore the disabled, here was an opportunity to be seen and heard. What a thrill to experience this empowering exercise in freedom of speech. Even though the three-day event was grueling for someone like me with a disease that saps every ounce of energy just by being awake, it was worth every effort.

I was asked to tell my story to the people we would be meeting with. I needed to keep it concise, talk about how ALS was affecting my life and my parents, and be specific about what I was requesting from the lawmakers. It wasn't difficult to pull everything together in the short time I was given, but I struggled to make it brief.

At every meeting we had on Capitol Hill, whether with the congresspeople themselves, such as Representatives Donald Payne Jr., Bob Menendez, and Mikie Sherrill, all three of them Democrats from New Jersey, or with one of their young and highly energetic aides, I shared my story by pressing play on the Tobii Dynavox speech generator computer mounted to my chair.

We fought for a number of policy initiatives on the Hill that day. The following outline gives context to the legislative challenges that we, the people who suffer from ALS, patients and caregivers alike, are facing:

Mission Statement

The ALS Association is focused on educating, advocating, and mobilizing all members of Congress in a bipartisan fashion to achieve the mission of the ALS Association: To discover treatments and a cure for ALS, and to serve, advocate for, and empower people affected by ALS to live their lives to the fullest.

Lead Initiatives

1. Waive the Five-Month Waiting Period for Social Security

The ALS Disability Insurance Access Act, to be introduced in the 116th Congress, will eliminate the five-month waiting period for Social Security Disability Insurance (SSDI). Under current law, people with ALS who qualify for SSDI must wait five months before receiving it and gaining access to Medicare. The legislation would eliminate the five-month waiting period for people with ALS.

2. *Preserve and Increase Federal Resources for ALS Research*
   Department of Defense (DOD). Provide at least a $20 million appropriation to continue the ALS Research Program (ALSRP) at the DOD. Research has repeatedly demonstrated that military veterans, regardless of branch or era of service, are approximately twice as likely to die from ALS than civilians. The ALSRP, funded as part of the Congressional Directed Medical Research Program at DOD, provides competitive grants that are an essential component of efforts to identify treatments and a cure for ALS.

   National ALS Registry. Provide a $10 million appropriation to continue with the National ALS Registry and Biorepository at the Centers for Disease Control and Prevention. The Registry, which collects and analyzes data and directs a Biorepository, works in close collaboration with the Centers for Medicare and Medicaid Services, the Veterans Administration, the DOD's ALS research program, and the National Institutes of Health (NIH).

   It is a critical driver of the search to find treatments and a cure because it connects researchers conducting clinical trials with people living with ALS and funds their own important research.

   National Institutes of Health. Continue ALS Research at the National Institute for Neurological Disorders and Stroke (NINDS) and other institutes at the NIH. In 2018, the NIH spent approximately $83 million on ALS research, with the NINDS making the largest investment and four other NIH institutes contributing to the balance.

The ALS Association will work in collaboration with other national organizations to advocate for $41.6 billion in funding for the NIH in 2019 (a $2.5 billion increase over 2018) to maintain and increase this level of commitment to ALS research.

3. *Access to Home Health Services*

Achievable policy solutions are needed to improve access to home health services for people living with ALS. The federal government's concerns about waste, fraud, and abuse of Medicare home health benefits for all seniors and misunderstandings about the scope of the benefit have significantly limited access for people living with ALS.

In 2019, the ALS Association will continue to educate and advocate with the administration and Congress on the home health needs of people with ALS, as well as identify achievable ways to remove barriers through regulatory and legislative action.

4. *Represent People Living with ALS on Access to Healthcare and Medications*

It is anticipated that both legislative and administrative proposals will be introduced that will impact access to healthcare and medications. The ALS Association will closely monitor and work with other patient advocacy groups to examine emerging proposals to determine their impact on people with ALS and their families.

Speaking with representatives from New Jersey was relatively simple since this is a blue state and the congresspeople we met with already supported these initiatives. For anyone with a shred of human dignity, these initiatives seem like no-brainers.

But some people don't have the same inherent compassion instilled in them from birth. Such was the case with Republican Senator Mike Lee from Utah. When he was asked why he wouldn't support these initiatives, he responded, "You are all on the dole."

This man needs to catch a quick case of whatever he's against. He has a number of options, considering he opposes disaster relief, funding for education, environmental protection, gun control, public health, LGBTQ rights, foreign and humanitarian aid, humane immigration policy, internet freedom, and, least surprisingly of all, racial equality.

Show me a man with an affliction and I'll show you a champion for a cause. Like Republican Senator Rob Portman from Ohio, who suddenly made an about-face on his stance on gay marriage when his son came out. Funny how that works. If the children of lawmakers were the first to be drafted into war, I'm fairly confident war would look much different.

To the folks we have elected and entrusted to vote on our behalf, become familiar with whatever causes you oppose. Dear Senator Mike Lee: I welcome you to spend one day in my chair and then cast your vote.

Being part of an advocacy effort gave me an appreciation of not only how poorly the government functions but also how laws are made. We're fortunate here in the United States that the average citizen has direct access to our representatives in the government. We can share our concerns and our wishes with them so they understand how our lives can improve if certain changes are made to the laws.

In December 2019, Congress reached an agreement to fully fund the spending priorities we had presented in June. A year later, the ALS Disability Insurance Access Act of 2019 was finally signed into law. People with ALS now have immediate access to SSDI and Medicare benefits. Our voices had been heard.

This is well within your reach as an average citizen. Once you have this experience, it's no longer acceptable to bitch and moan about the benefits or services you're not receiving from the government, or how you're being treated by a company. Write a letter, send an email or tweet, or volunteer with an advocacy organization. However you decide to get involved, choose not to be invisible.

19

You Are Your Best Advocate

KIRSTEN COCOMAN, PRESIDENT AND CEO of the ALS Association of Greater New York and Greater Philadelphia Chapters, reached out in early March 2020. She asked if I would give my testimony to the New Jersey State Senate Budget Commission to help secure funding for the ALS Association for the 2020–2021 budget year.

Without asking what was involved, I immediately said yes. She asked on a Thursday, and the meeting was scheduled for the following Tuesday. During a brief call, Kristen gave me a rundown of what she wanted to accomplish at the meeting, who I would present to, and what my testimony should include.

Kristen's communication director sent me a copy of the previous year's testimony as a guide to help me structure mine. When I found out that every nonprofit in New Jersey would be at this hearing asking for money, I tossed it in the circular filing bin under my desk.

If I was tasked with making the "Big Ask" in the allotted time of three minutes, I needed to tell a compelling story. The draft I received read like the bylaws of a company—it lacked emotion and a compelling call to action.

The version I presented had a monster (ALS) that terrorized the town (people with ALS), a weapon to fight the monster ($1 million for the Greater New York and Greater Philadelphia Chapters), and a hero (the New Jersey State Budget Commission) to save us from the monster.

During my career in sales, $1 million wasn't an uncommon price tag for the products I sold (think MRI machines and X-ray equipment to hospitals and software to global banks). Now, I was preparing for the most important sale of my life. Each person and caregiver affected by ALS in New Jersey and Philadelphia depended on me, as did the ALS Association Greater New York and Greater Philadelphia Chapters.

The commission held the meeting at the New Jersey Institute of Technology. After my parents and I arrived, we signed in, took our seats, and waited to be called up to the podium. The auditorium was practically empty—not a surprise considering the country was about to go into lockdown due to the coronavirus. The nonprofits that did show up rightly assumed they would be facing less competition and would thus stand out from the crowd.

When I was called up to the microphone, my father set up my computer. Debbie Schlossberg, social worker extraordinaire, sat on my left, ready to field questions from the panel of senators.

A convenient little perk of this disease is the ability to record anything I want to say on my little speech device and play it back later. I can zip right past the stage fright and sweaty palms and get straight to the point. Barring any unintentional and potentially offensive mispronunciations, my only job is to sit there and look pretty.

Once I was all set up, I hit play. Over the next four minutes and thirty-two seconds, I watched the bar mitzvah–sized dais of senators perk up and lean forward, hanging on every synthesized word. Since I was sitting there with nothing to do, I swiveled my head, scanning the room to gauge the impact of my testimony.

My full testimony:

Dear Members of the New Jersey Senate Budget Committee:

Thank you for the opportunity to be here today. My name is Jeremy Schreiber. I live in Livingston, New Jersey, represented by Senator Richard Codey. I am forty years old. When I was thirty-eight, I was diagnosed with ALS.

When I got my diagnosis, it was a shock to us because we have no family history of ALS. In fact, 90 percent of the people diagnosed do not either. Just like cancer, it can happen to anyone. And if you are a military veteran, you are twice as likely to get ALS, regardless of what branch you served in or where you were deployed.

In the aftermath of my diagnosis, we held each other and cried. We did this because we knew it was a death sentence. Because there is no cure.

ALS is a progressive disease, killing the nerves throughout our bodies. Like Lou Gehrig and Stephen Hawking before me, I have lost my ability to walk, to use my hands, to eat, to talk, and eventually, I will lose my ability to breathe.

This computer speaks for me while I sit in this wheelchair because my body is failing me. I am not unique. This is the course everyone with ALS will suffer. Unfortunately, the parts of our bodies that are spared are our eyes and our minds.

I say "unfortunately" because those of us with ALS are fully aware of what is happening to us while we are forced to watch the pain this disease causes our family and friends. And there is nothing we can do.

I am here to be the voice of the thousands of other New Jersey residents with ALS who are confined to their homes, dependent on ventilators and feeding tubes, and for many of whom travel is impossible.

I am also here to thank you on behalf of the ALS Association Greater New York and Greater Philadelphia Chapters for approving $250,000 last year in the New Jersey State Budget. That funding was split between the two chapters in the state.

Because of New Jersey's commitment to supporting people like me and families like mine, the ALS Association is able to help manage the overwhelming medical and financial needs that arise from this disease. Specifically from past budget support, the Greater New York Chapter was able to hire a new full-time care services coordinator in New Jersey, who has been essential to the organization's growth.

The coordinator has increased the chapter's reach into previously underserved areas, the number of people with ALS served, and the number of services provided regionally, including home visits, transportation, and equipment loaned, which are provided at no cost to the patient or family.

Because there is no cure, my family and I, along with others around New Jersey struggling with ALS, depend on the services the ALS Association provides. Many of us who are diagnosed are sent home with a stack of pamphlets, a time limit of two to five years to live, and instructions to get our affairs in order.

Your decision to continue funding the requests of the ALS Association has allowed us to rewrite that story by providing expert resources and support I can count on, equipment I can borrow to ease the financial burden, and a community I can lean on.

Given the increased needs of the ALS population and urgency of care, the ALS Association is respectfully asking for $1 million in the fiscal year 2021 budget. With increased funding, the Greater New York Chapter plans to do the following:

- Hire another full-time care services coordinator to provide additional home visits and supportive services to PALS [People with ALS] in New Jersey, focusing on underserved regions.
- Grow a transportation program to provide PALS with transport to support groups and chapter events, like research symposia and the Walk to Defeat ALS.
- Expand the equipment loan program to add high-cost durable medical equipment and augmentative communication devices that are regularly requested by patients but are too expensive at this time.
- Add specialty support groups throughout the region.
- Provide additional grants to PALS and their families for home and respite care.

> The funding we hope this panel will provide the ALS Association this year means those of us who have ALS in New Jersey can start living with the disease and stop dying from it.
>
> I am truly grateful for the opportunity to speak to you today and thank you for your consideration.

Not a dry eye in the house. After finishing my testimony, we packed up and drove home. Such an incredible experience and one I would absolutely do again given the chance.

I caught bits and pieces from the organization that presented after me. They were asking for the elimination of the luxury tax on yachts purchased in New Jersey. I'm all for advocacy for your cause, but they might have considered presenting before me to avoid having their message be compared with mine.

In the summer of 2020, we found out that our request for the million dollars had been approved.

If something bothers you, make your voice heard by telling the decision-makers exactly what you need them to do.

• • •

Nothing makes me feel more subhuman than dealing with customer service. Frankly, nothing makes me want to commit homicide more than that. Those who work in customer service have one job: Fix the customer's problem as quickly as possible and move on to the next schmuck waiting in line.

The same is especially true in healthcare. When was the last time you visited your doctor and he or she had plenty of time to hang around and chat with you? I spent a decade on the sales side of the healthcare industry working with providers at all sorts of levels. What I can tell you for sure is that these poor people don't have time to take a shit let alone spend quality time with their patients.

Why are they so busy? It's fairly simple. Way back when doctors were considered one step below God, they began to charge higher and higher fees, surely to cover their loans and medical malpractice insurance, as well as turning a profit.

Enter stage right, the large insurance companies, like the one your employer might provide. We will call them the Big Bad Wolf. Through your paycheck, you pay a little to the Big Bad Wolf, your employer pays a little more to the Big Bad Wolf, and the Big Bad Wolf pays the doctor. As insurance companies gain more control and medicine becomes more of a commodity, the amount the Big Bad Wolf pays the doctor goes down. But we still expect the doctor to cure cancer for the ninety dollars they receive for our visit.

There's more to the plight of the physician, but the story doesn't get better. Add in the complexity and expense of the electronic medical record system, a grumpy staff, and, of course, the drug rep.

I should know—I was the well-dressed guy in a suit, carrying a bag of goodies for the staff and samples for the doctor. My goal was to get the doctor to see me, the rep, before you, the patient. After all, if you had a doctor's appointment in the middle of the workday, chances are you had nowhere else to be, right? Whatever it was I had to tell the doctor was certainly worth three minutes of everyone's time. If I happened to be peddling something that worked better than whatever you were taking, wouldn't that make the interruption worthwhile?

So how, as an individual with complex needs, are you supposed to get the attention you so badly need? Think about all the stories about celebrities throwing Hiroshima-sized temper tantrums because their dog, Fluffy, was served store-bought dog food instead of fresh roasted chicken. What happens? That gets everyone's attention, doesn't it?

Be careful, though, this is a one-time use technique. There are many more-diplomatic ways of getting what you want without appearing like a Kardashian.

Here are some tips:

- Use LinkedIn or Google to find the highest-level person you can that sounds relevant, such as head of customer service, chief patient experience officer, or chief medical officer.
- Go to the home page of the facility and look for the names of corporate officers.
- Find the email format used by the organization.
- Email everyone using the template below.
- Remember to always be respectful.

Example email template:

Subject: Patient in need of help

Dear ____________,

My name is__________________. I was diagnosed with ____________________ and have been a patient in your ____________________ facility. I am reaching out to ask for your help.

I have been working with the __________ department on _______________. For some reason, the progress in getting me the ____________ I need has come to a grinding halt. I have been unable to reach the practitioners in these groups after multiple attempts over the last month.

Unfortunately, my condition is progressing rapidly, and I desperately need these things sooner rather than later. I would really appreciate your help in clearing the roadblocks I am encountering.

_______________, thank you in advance for your help and attention to this. I am happy to answer any questions you might have.

Gratefully,

____

When you're handed a diagnosis with a countdown timer, suddenly everything becomes urgent, and this needs to be impressed upon all the people you meet in a position of service. Even when your lousy customer service experience has nothing to do with improving your health, going to the top is sometimes the only way to get things done.

I purchased a new trackball mouse directly from Logitech for my computer, thinking my rapidly deforming hands could use this style more easily. But I couldn't maneuver my clenching fingers and stiffening wrist well enough around the mouse, so I needed to return it. Should be simple enough. Just look in the box for the return label.

Okay, no label. No problem. I would print it from the Logitech site. Funny, the site had no "returns" area. All I could find was a link to the live chat agent.

After a forty-five-minute wait, I was still ninth in the queue. Absurd. I pressed every combination of options, but the 800 number yielded no live person. Time to turn to the support forums. Apparently, I wasn't alone in my frustration. Page after page of complaints about how difficult the return process was from soon-to-be ex-customers begging for help.

That was when I deployed the steps outlined above. Wouldn't you know it? Twelve hours later, I received an email from customer service apologizing for all the trouble and sending a postage-paid return label. At the bottom of that email, I saw my original email to the top brass at Logitech with directions for this customer service agent to help me. Mission accomplished.

What about my frustrated friends on the forums who needed to return their products and were struggling like I was? Not wanting anyone else to endure more pain inflicted by this soul-crushing corporate giant, I posted my methodology, along with the contact information of those customer experience executives who were so helpful in resolving my return difficulties.

When you're forced to become invisible, make your voice heard by going straight to the top.

20

Raising Money

BEING SICK CAN SHRINK YOUR WORLD. If social distancing and self-isolation during the coronavirus pandemic made you stir crazy, you just caught a glimpse of life with a chronic illness or disability.

Fortunately, organizations supporting people who have an illness or disability understand the need to create communities that foster inclusion. Even though getting involved with these organizations means you'll hear about the struggle that others with your condition are facing, it helped me find purpose and a reason to get out of bed.

As I got more involved, my mood improved, I was less depressed, and I began to feel better. Being part of a community has given me ideas on how to help my parents and tremendous satisfaction in helping others.

Remember, just because you're sick, you don't have to feel sick. A positive attitude will carry you a long way.

I had no idea so many people in my life cared about me. It was amazing when they came forward and offered to help. Their outstanding creativity blew me away, as did their willingness to work hard on my behalf.

Support came in many forms beyond money. The men of MDI, realizing how difficult it was for me to travel to the weekly meeting, committed to hosting one meeting a month at my house. Every time they came over, they made a point of finding something my parents needed help with around the house and did it for them. They organized the garage, built a closet, and fixed a broken Wi-Fi router, to name a few.

Our traditional fundraisers exceeded all our expectations. Patrick McCartney and Laura Hickey launched an incredible GoFundMe campaign that helped me get the equipment I needed to make our lives easier: the accessible van, an overhead ceiling hoist to transfer me out of bed and into the bathroom, and some experimental medicine from overseas.

Darren and Molly Manning of the Tim Sheehey Softball Classic made some important introductions to people and resources that I'm grateful for. Meanwhile, Project Main Street invited me as their guest of honor at their annual benefit concert in Brooklyn.

Melissa pulled together an outstanding cabaret at Don't Tell Momma in NYC, packing the house with talented professional performers and friends I missed so much. She also enlisted the help of her friend Camille Torres to create an inspirational cuff-style bracelet with the engraved quote: "You are stronger than you seem, and you are braver than you believe." We sold them at the second annual MDI Ugly "Schweater" Benefit Concert at the Rockwood Music Hall in Manhattan.

None of these events were difficult to arrange. All it took was a few motivated friends and some brainstorming.

If you're interested in passively contributing to a nonprofit organization important to you, Amazon has created Amazon Smile. Shop as you normally would, and a portion of the price of the item you purchase is donated to the company of your choice. I chose the

ALS Therapy Development Institute. Go to smile.amazon.com, log in with your regular Amazon username and password, and you'll be prompted to select a nonprofit. Ask your friends and family to do the same.

Celebrity status comes with certain responsibilities, and each person achieving that status, whether by choice or chance, must respect everything that comes with it. One such celebrity, Steve Gleason, former NFL quarterback for the New Orleans Saints, uses the podium for the greater good.

Diagnosed with ALS in 2011, Steve has not only lived with this disease but also thrived. He wants to inspire others to do the same. Steve and his wife, Michel, formed the nonprofit organization Team Gleason to help him accomplish that goal and more. He has played an instrumental role in passing two laws and creating new technologies for people with ALS and other disabilities. For his extraordinary efforts, he was awarded the Congressional Gold Medal.

Part of Team Gleason's commitment to helping those with ALS is to send them on a once-in-a-lifetime trip anywhere they want to go. I took Melissa, Todd, and his wife, Sandy, to Grand Cayman for a week. No words can adequately express my gratitude for that unforgettable experience.

After the meteoric success of our GoFundMe campaign, I received a flood of questions from people who wanted to set up their own campaign. So I asked Laura and Patrick to share their secrets.

In Laura's own words:

> We started a GoFundMe campaign for Jeremy when we heard about his diagnosis. Based on our experience, here are some tips for anyone considering a crowdfunding campaign:

1. *Let go of your reservations.*

It's easy to feel helpless when you or a loved one falls ill or faces unexpected hardship. Many of us struggle with asking for help from others. Whether you are starting a campaign for yourself or for someone else, when you have decided to ask for help, own it.

Many people in your life and the world care about you and humanity at large. Dig deep and be prepared as an advocate, cheerleader, and solicitor. The process can seem overwhelming at times, but if you approach it with the right mindset from the beginning, you'll find that some parts are actually not that difficult to tackle.

2. *Research your options.*

Before we decided to set up the GoFundMe campaign, we kicked around several ideas about how to raise money for Jeremy. Coworkers wanted to help, but no one was sure of the best course of action.

We chose crowdfunding for several reasons: ease of use, the option to donate using a credit card, the possibility of sharing across multiple social media platforms, and the immediate availability of funds.

GoFundMe isn't the only option, so research, read the fine print, and make a choice depending on your goals and reasons for starting a campaign. Because GoFundMe is a well-known and trusted platform, user-friendly, and relatively low-cost for medical campaigns, we believed it was the best way to get something off the ground quickly. Whichever platform you use, download its app, if available.

3. *Set a reasonable initial goal.*

Talk about needs with family and others involved, the minimum amount you're comfortable with, and what you think is realistically achievable. Be as specific as possible in your request about what the money will be used for.

GoFundMe campaigns don't expire, and you can change the goal as needed. I promise that reaching the initial goal and increasing it is better for your psyche than starting out with a high amount and never achieving it.

4. *Write like your life depends on it (it probably does).*
At first, your campaign will be focused on your immediate network, so you may think that your story is partially understood. Write it for those who don't know you at all and make it as personal and compelling as possible. Include details of your life before and after whatever prompted your campaign, and how donations will change your situation.

If you're starting a campaign for someone else, collaborate to get all the information that person wants to include. Take your time, write well, and proofread.

Keep in mind that those sharing your campaign are just as important as those donating, and any stranger you can get to do either is a bonus. Trending campaigns that are shared across multiple social media platforms are seen by many people you have never met, and you want them to want to help.

5. *Hit the pavement.*
It would be wonderful if I could say that once you go live with your campaign, your work is done and you will easily meet your goal. The truth is that many campaigns struggle to be fully funded.

When you launch, be ready to share across all your social media accounts, utilize community Facebook groups, and direct message people to personally ask them to share.

Work your network, however big or small. If your campaign is for someone else, include them and their family in the effort if you can. If at all possible, try to launch your campaign around a public event (a party, benefit, service) and be ready to talk about it.

I hurried to get our campaign ready before my husband went to several days of company-wide meetings. While I was working on things behind the scenes, he was talking about the campaign to everyone at those meetings, over and over.

Old-school face time is important, and the more people you can ask to talk about your situation the better. Take your campaign with you to work, church, school, clubs, and social gatherings. I always asked people to share the campaign, even if I didn't bring up donating directly.

6. *Update often.*

Once people start donating and sharing, they will receive notifications of anything you post. Additional information, changes in the situation, expressions of gratitude, or updates on your goal are important to those who are invested in your well-being.

They want to hear from you, and ongoing communication helps encourage more sharing and donations. If appropriate to the situation, you can add others as administrators so they can post updates as well.

Understandably, Jeremy and his family had trouble staying on top of everything at first, so we posted the updates but also added him so he could post when he could. As time progressed, he was able to take the reins and let everyone know about benefits and other events via the campaign.

7. *Write a personal thank-you note.*

GoFundMe sends a thank-you form anytime someone donates, but you have the option to send a personalized one.

Take the opportunity for a heartfelt thank-you in your own words and change it accordingly.

For example, when we updated the goal to help pay for a van or a specific treatment, I included it in my thank-you to anyone donating after that update. I changed my thank-you around the holidays to wish donors well during the season.

The app makes it easy to keep track of who has donated and who you have thanked. You can set a template to do this with one click. When you're getting a lot of donations, monitoring them can be time consuming, but it's worth it. I have made personal connections with people who have set up recurring donations and had others reach out to me with various ideas and desires to help.

8. Beware.

Scammers contacted us through Facebook and Instagram claiming they could increase traffic to the campaign for money. No matter how desperate your circumstances, do not fall victim to this.

Also, and especially if your campaign is trending, you may see comments on your campaign from bots promoting questionable medical advice and from people trying to direct you to their own campaigns. Use care and discretion to cull these from your comments if you wish. Ultimately, I decided to delete any comment that wasn't positive.

Starting the campaign for Jeremy was one of our greatest honors. It is heartening to see support from so many people and restores some of our faith in the world. As hard as it is to face tragedy or illness, I encourage you to turn outward and ask for help (monetary, social, spiritual) when you need it.

A bright spot in an otherwise hopeless-feeling situation can make all the difference.

21

Everyone Has to Get Involved

MY INTENTION IN WRITING THIS book wasn't simply to tell my story and gain your sympathy. Yes, it's been a huge struggle as you have read, but how many others have been through perhaps even worse? And what worries me is how many more will have to suffer tomorrow and the next day because the organizations with power and money choose to do what's popular instead of what's right.

This is not only a book about ALS written for people suffering with the disease. It's a book for everyone, for people with any type of disability, but also for able-bodied people and those in positions of power within local, state, and federal government organizations. While we in the disabled community have a large role to play in improving society so we're no longer invisible, it's the whole of society that needs to get involved. We can't do this alone.

The ADA should be the answer to our needs, but let's face it, the law sucks! What the ADA designates as accessible is rarely usable in practice. If professionals designing buildings and other structures decide to take any real notice of the ADA, how often do they actually talk to people with disabilities? I would suggest hardly ever, if at all, from my experience.

And the ADA is outdated. It attempts to address website and mobile app usability but doesn't enforce anything. These weak regulations contribute to our invisibility—even though we have a wealth of knowledge that could help designers make all public spaces, digital properties included, accessible to everyone, regardless of ability. Until the government rewrites the ADA to ensure that disabled people are consulted, the status quo will continue.

Of course, it's not just about buildings and websites. It's about people. And we need people to change things so obviously wrong.

If you are able-bodied, you may feel uncomfortable around someone with a disability and not know how to act, but understand that the awkwardness you feel is a learned behavior. So is racism, homophobia, and xenophobia. And we as a society have managed to (mostly) eliminate those horrible warts from our lives. That means the responsibility for eliminating the exclusion of people who are different from you falls squarely on your shoulders.

Teach your children the Golden Rule—remind them of its importance when they enter the workforce and then again when they have children of their own. Just how difficult can it be to look us in the eye and talk to us as adults? I can assure you that it would make me feel a hell of a lot better, and it would change the way your children perceive you. I take the burden of speaking on behalf of the vast majority of people with disabilities when I say that.

To everyone who reads this book, I hope my story inspires you to be the best version of yourself. Those of you in situations like mine, I challenge you to take control of your lives. Use the tools I've presented to become your own advocate for your health.

And if you're fortunate enough to be an outsider to life-changing illnesses and disabilities, I challenge you to acknowledge a behavior that you have seen from another person, or that you might be guilty of yourself, and make a concerted effort to change it—to be better.

The sixty million of us with disabilities in the United States can't live our lives as we would like, but it's up to us to make our lives as fulfilling as we can. A lot can be done if we fight for the right to be counted, to be heard—not pushed to the shadows of the very society we help build.

Choose to be visible. Don't simply accept what is. Think about what you need, what you can do for yourself, but also what you need others to do for you. If we all do this together, we can make a change.

Publisher's note: Thank you for reading *Never Say Invisible.* We are eager to raise awareness for ALS, as well as for the millions of people struggling with disabilities. Please help us spread the word about Jeremy's story by posting a rating and short review on Amazon and Goodreads. We look forward to your comments and thank you again for all your support.

Amazon

Goodreads

Acknowledgments

From Jeremy's parents, Fred and Ronnye Schreiber:

Usually the author writes the acknowledgments, but our dear son, Jeremy, is no longer with us and didn't get the chance to write that section. Since we don't know everyone involved in creating and promoting his book, we probably have unknowingly omitted some. Our apologies.

Augusten Burroughs. Thank you for the beautiful foreword and for your ongoing emails with Jeremy that always brightened his day.

Todd Adest. Todd introduced Jeremy to MDI, the men's group that helped him cope with ALS and other issues. He and his wife, Sandy, have stayed with us through every step of this horrible disease. Thank you for letting us continue to be a part of your family.

Laura Hickey and Patrick McCarthy. Laura and Patrick created the GoFundMe site for Jeremy. Laura is continuing to keep the site active and the proceeds from donations are now going to help offset book-marketing costs. These folks continue to be a very important part of our lives.

Melissa Simpson. Jeremy's very significant other reviewed the book, helped with the cover, and always kept his spirits up. Thanks for always being there for Jeremy.

Sebastian and Michelle Reichelt. Best man at his wedding and friends for life, Sebastian helped us understand the influencer process and how we could promote the book. He also ran NYC marathons to support ALS and had Jeremy's name on his pinnie.

MDI: Mentor, Discover, and Inspire. This international organization that made a difference in Jeremy's life and is helping us promote the book globally. They bought his push wheelchair early on when he fell and was injured, and were always there to support him.

Sandra Jonas, of Sandra Jonas Publishing. Sandra picked up the pieces from Jeremy's book project after he passed away and brought the project to fruition. I would coin the term "forensic publishing" for the enormous amount of detective work she did to uncover the multiple components that Jeremy had brought together (and that were nearly lost to us after his passing) to get his book out there. Thank you.

Jeremy's parents, Fred and Ronnye. We scoured Jeremy's computer after his passing to hunt for all the websites and services and personalities that he used to create his book. This was a challenge for us non-techies, but worth the effort!

We thank his friends Gillad and Dassi Matiteyahu, Julie Cohen, Heidi Reynders, Meredith Remz, Lauren Weber, and Rachel Smolney, as well as his former classmates, former coworkers, and his MDI group for everything they did to make his time with us as cheerful and meaningful as possible. To the celebrities who endorsed the book, we really appreciate your help. You have all added to our wonderful memories of Jeremy.

Photo Album

April 2018. Jeremy in Cabo San Lucas soon after his diagnosis.

July 2018. An MDI 5K event that Jeremy organized.

June 2018. Jeremy and his mother, Ronnye, in NYC. Jeremy was still using forearm crutches then.

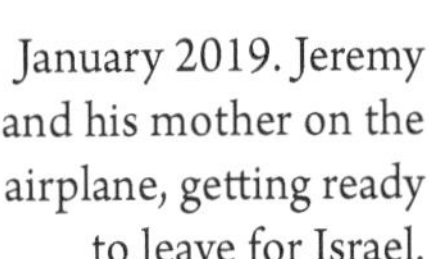

January 2019. Jeremy and his mother on the airplane, getting ready to leave for Israel.

January 2019. Jeremy and his father, Fred, during their trip to Israel.

January 2019. Jeremy in the family Scooby mobile.

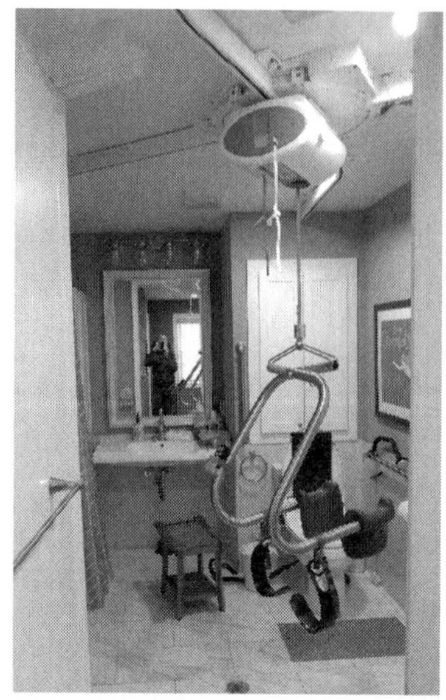

March 2019. Renovations: the bathroom ceiling lift and turntable.

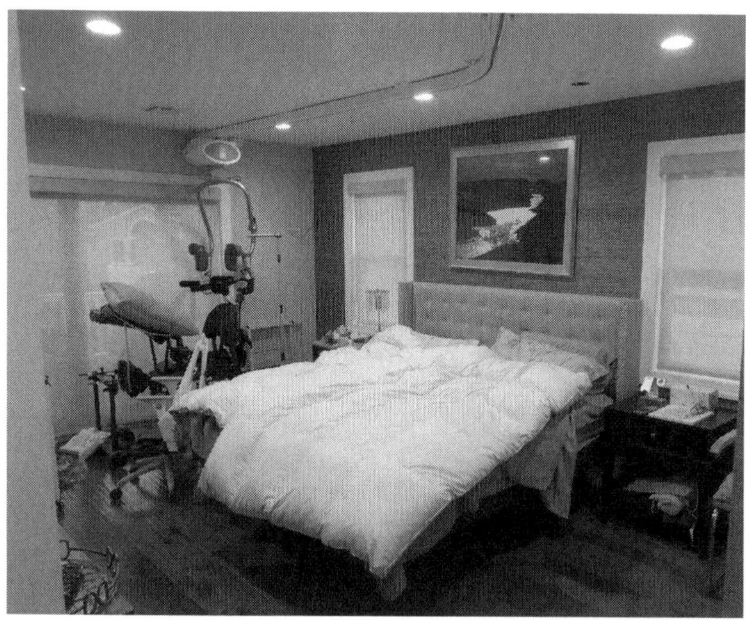

March 2019. Renovations: the bedroom ceiling track and lift.

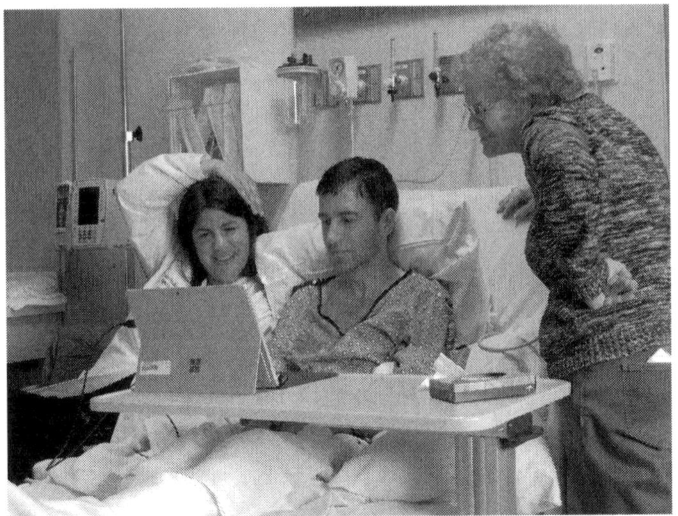

May 2019. Clinical trial at the University of Massachusetts Medical School in Worcester.

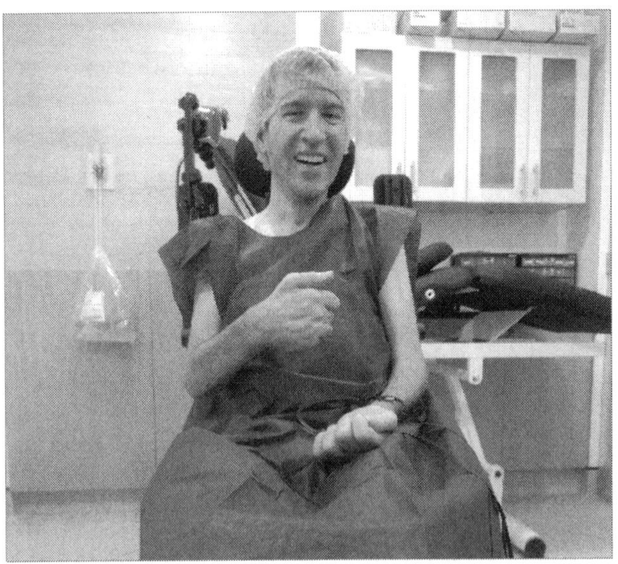

October 2019. Stem Cell Transplant Institute, San Jose, Costa Rica. Jeremy is trying to give a thumbs-up.

June 2019. Jeremy, his mother (*left*), and two attendees at the ALS Advocacy Conference in Washington, DC.

June 2019. Jeremy and Katrina Hawking, daughter-in-law to the late Stephen Hawking, on ALS Advocacy Day in Washington, DC.

October 2019. *From left to right*: Sandy and Todd Adest, Melissa, Jeremy, Cap'n Ron, and Ron's sidekick with stingrays in Stingray City (the Team Gleason Grand Cayman trip).

January 2020. Melissa and Jeremy on their way to see Steve Cohen's *Chamber Magic* show in NYC.

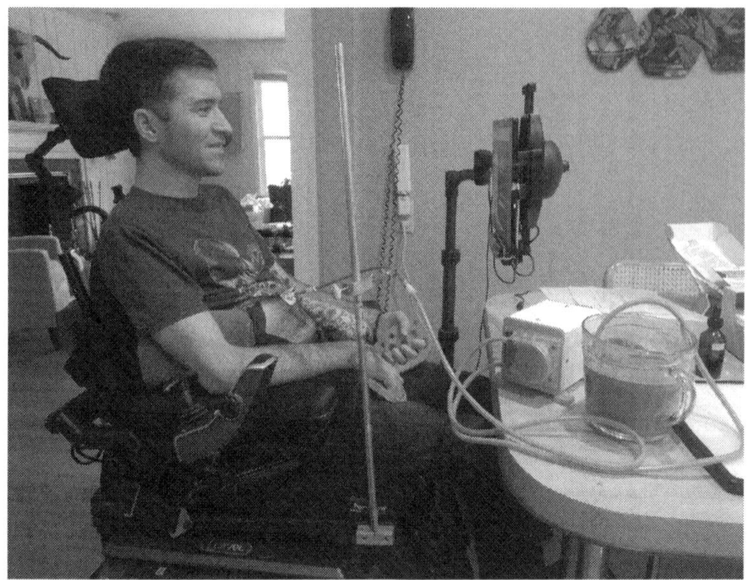

March 2020. Jeremy's feeding-tube setup. His father made hand splints for him to keep his fingers from contracting.

March 2020. Jeremy with his parents after he testified at the New Jersey Senate Budget and Appropriations Committee hearing on behalf of the ALS Association.

Building Your Guide to Thrive

Jeremy developed this valuable, detailed resource for anyone hit with a life-altering health condition or injury:

You have an overwhelmingly difficult and energy-sapping cross to bear. Give yourself sufficient time to grieve, but put a limit on the process. It doesn't serve anyone by spending your days under the covers dripping in a week of stench. Get out of bed, wash up, and go outside. You need to face the music. Your life won't get any better by avoiding the situation.

Now that you're over that, make a plan for how you're going to master your new life.

Your "Guide to Thrive" will be a manual for you and your caregivers to live by. It will include everything necessary to take care of you day to day. Whether you can do that yourself or you need some assistance, it's important to get organized, especially if you plan on beating the dealer at his own game.

What keeps me going is knowing I'm in control and that I would rather live with ALS than die from it.

CRAFTING YOUR GUIDE

You can use any tool you're comfortable with to keep your protocol organized. I'm a fan of Evernote, but Microsoft Word or Google Docs works just as well. You can use a notebook, though with the frequent changes, an electronic document will make your life easier. Keeping this online also allows you to share it with anyone else who might be interested.

Whatever tool you choose, make sure your Guide to Thrive is easily accessible. If it's difficult to use or find, it will end up going the way of that treadmill sitting in your den.

WHAT TO INCLUDE

By now you have probably thumbed through these pages and said "Fuck it" when you saw all the things I'm suggesting you include in your protocol. I don't blame you. But please know that mine was created piece by piece over several months and continues to evolve.

Contact List

Of course, you have each number you need neatly stored in your phone, but the one time you're not near your phone in an emergency, who would think to look for your cardiologist under *S* for "Smokin' hot doc"?

If you're tech savvy enough, use a tool like Asana or Trello. You can keep all your important contacts in there and share it with your family so they can simply search for "cardiologist."

Your list should include not only your doctor's details, but also anyone who treats you—the home health agency, acupuncturist, shaman, pharmacy, witch doctor, and others. You could even include the name of your "guy" in case you run out of your favorite illicit drug. Not that I'm recommending it.

Your Diagnosis or Disability

Obvious to you, but you would be surprised how many people, caregiver wannabes, well-intentioned friends, and HHAs don't have a clue what's wrong with you or how to work with your new limitations.

Add a brief description of your condition in layman's terms, as well as anything important about the way it affects you. For example, your right arm doesn't bend easily, or bright lights cause you pain, or your mother-in-law slows the healing process.

Drugs, Supplements, and Vitamins

You'll be asked about the medications you're taking more times than you can imagine, so keep them organized. When I go to my appointments, I hand a printout of the list to the receptionist along with my insurance card.

Often overlooked, though just as important as prescribed medications, are any vitamins or supplements you're taking. It might seem pointless, since you don't need a prescription to buy them, but that's the exact reason you should tell your caregivers and doctors everything you take.

From the FDA ("Mixing Medications and Dietary Supplements Can Endanger Your Health"):

> Combining dietary supplements and medications could have dangerous and even life-threatening effects. For example, drugs for HIV/AIDS, heart disease, depression, treatments for organ transplants, and birth control pills are less effective when taken with St. John's Wort, an herbal supplement. Depending on the medication involved, the results can be serious.
>
> In addition, warfarin (a prescription blood thinner), ginkgo biloba (an herbal supplement), aspirin, and vitamin E (a supplement) can each thin the blood. Taking any of these products together may increase the potential for internal bleeding or stroke.

I hope you agree that this is important and you'll include all your supplements in your guide.

Alternative Treatments

This section is useful for all the non-Western medicine and treatments you're trying. Things like acupuncture, yoga, sensory deprivation or float tanks, cupping, bloodletting, exorcism, home trepanning, electroshock therapy, or anything else your doctor doesn't have a clue about and is probably unwilling to discuss.

Recently, marijuana has come back into question as playing a role in patients requiring higher doses of anesthesia during surgery. Don't worry about disclosing your pot habit. I assure you that no one cares.

Physical and Occupational Therapies

Typically, physical and occupational therapies are provided for a limited amount of time by your insurance company. This is your opportunity to learn (soak up) everything you possibly can.

Bring someone with you to take notes, or better yet take a video. The objective is to continue the work at home. Ask the therapist how best to group the exercises. You can include pictures or drawings, but make sure to add descriptions of each exercise in your own words.

Participation in Clinical Trials

While exploring treatment options, you'll surely come across clinical trials for your condition. The decision to participate is entirely yours. You'll have to weigh the benefits against the risks, taking into account such factors as the phase of the trial, travel requirements, and out-of-pocket expenses. I'm in favor of participating in the right trial at the appropriate time.

Simply put, you already know how your condition affects you without treatment, or with the treatments you're already on. When properly selected, a clinical trial could make a huge improvement in your life. Working together with your doctor, sharing the pertinent details of the trial and the risks, will help you decide if the trial is right for you:

- Name of the trial
- Phase 1, 2, or 3?
- Lead investigator
- URL to the ClinicalTrials.gov entry
- Location of the study center nearest to you
- Frequency of visits to the study center
- Potential out-of-pocket costs (gas, hotels, meals)

This is a good time to write down questions for your doctor. Here are a few suggestions:

- What do you know about this trial?
- Do you know the lead investigators? If yes, and I decide to enroll, will you reach out to them and ask that I'm enrolled right away?
- Do you have any patients participating in it? What feedback have they given you? Can I speak with them about their experience?
- Do I meet the inclusion criteria? If not, what can we do to help me meet them?
- What makes me a good or bad candidate?
- If I were to enroll in this trial, what are your concerns?
- What risks should I be aware of?
- What other trials should I consider?
- What haven't I asked that I should?

Participating in a clinical trial isn't an easy decision, especially if you're not well versed in the nuances of how a trial works. This is why you should talk with your doctor before enrolling.

Unapproved Treatments or Treatments for Ongoing Trials

The beauty of the internet is the ability to connect with people in similar situations around the world. I frequently use a website called PatientsLikeMe.com. There, I met a community of others with ALS and was introduced to treatments I might not have otherwise heard about.

For example, after hearing about CuATSM, Ibudilast, Leap2BeFit, and stem cell therapies, I did a tremendous amount of research into the claims I heard, the science behind the treatment, and how to get my hands on them.

Though probably not the best idea, Melissa tries everything first. That's fine for the ceiling hoist and breathing machines, but trying the homogeneous-colored, gruel-mix medicine and blended food might be taking it a bit far.

Oh, the things we do for love.

Food and Food Preferences

Hopefully, your condition won't affect your ability to eat the foods you love in the way you always have. But in many cases, ALS included, eating normally becomes a distant memory. If you're lucky, your doctor will slap your hand and tell you to cut out salt. If your condition is more serious, keep reading.

For me, as with many people, food has an emotional connection to family and friends, events, and memories and is an important way to share experiences. To maintain that connection, try not to deviate from the foods you love as best as possible.

This is the right time to get a nutritionist involved. Nutritionists or dietitians can develop a meal plan that preserves your current eating habits and preferences, and make any necessary adjustments. Pull the following information together and email it before your appointment. Your nutritionist will then have constructive suggestions on the day you meet.

Preferences

What do you enjoy eating? I love a greasy mushroom and Swiss burger medium rare, with Sriracha and a side of crispy fries. Don't forget the extra dirty Hendrick's martini in a rocks glass, obviously. You should be that specific.

Tolerability

What things do you have trouble tolerating? For example, red sauce gives you heartburn, or you can only tolerate one particular type of feeding tube formula, or anything your mother-in-law serves makes you sick.

Allergies

Important! List any food allergies and what happens when you encounter those items. For example, you have a peanut allergy and go into anaphylaxis whenever you touch anything with peanuts. Or you're afraid your mother-in-law is trying to poison you by hiding shellfish in your soup.

The more you share with your nutritionist, the easier it will be to craft a meal plan that works for you. I know what you're thinking: *I'm not going on a diet.* This isn't a diet in the traditional sense of the word. When your life is changed involuntarily, the way you used to do things will also change.

THE BIG PICTURE

Make good use of your care team. If you want them to prioritize you in their busy practice, engage them in the process of completing the sections above. That way you come up with an actionable plan for everyone to follow.

ALSisms

You know ALS is a silly disease when . . .

- You can have a frozen margarita, but water is off limits.
- A sock in your hand at night provides comfort.
- You have repurposed every device in your house as a positioning aid.
- Your power chair selects your caregivers by behaving erratically around the bad aides.
- Towels become a hot commodity in your house.
- Your wife folds laundry on top of you because it's easier than getting you out of bed.
- My girlfriend knows all my favorite positions . . . of my limbs.
- You always get stuck as the rock when playing rock, paper, scissors.
- You're exempt from chores because your [insert body part] doesn't work.
- Prepositions are removed from your vocabulary.
- ALS as a verb is easier for your friends to understand than explaining what's actually happening.
- Your formula is more appetizing than your caregiver's coronavirus back-of-the-freezer concoction.

- Your caregivers stop guessing what you said and start alphabetically listing body parts you want wiped.
- You suffer through the tenth iteration of that same damn story because it takes too long to type: "We heard that one already, Dad!"
- When the same parent who grounded you in high school for this transgression is helping you vape marijuana daily. (Debbie Schlossberg)
- Your first power chair with monster wheels and a truck horn is used daily to chase the dogs in the yard. An ALS sport. (Terri Handler)
- You forget it's not normal to turn off light switches with your forehead. (Erin Hines)
- When your power chair goes rogue and attacks your caregiver. (Robert Abernathy)
- You learn how to endure an itch until the feeling goes away. (Tee Fischer and Kenice Freeman)

Resources

Here are the resources found throughout the book. More are available on Jeremy's blog: neversayinvisible.com/blog.

- ALS Association: als.org
- ALS Therapy Development Institute: als.net
- ALSUntangled: alsuntangled.com
- Amazon Smile: smile.amazon.com
- Camille Torres Designs: camilletorresdesigns.com
- Jason Becker Vocal Eyes: jasonbecker.com/archive/VocalEyesCommunicate.pdf
- Jeremy's GoFundMe campaign: gofundme.com/f/HelpJeremyFightALS
- Mentor Discover Inspire: mentordiscoverinspire.org
- PatientsLikeMe: patientslikeme.com
- Search for clinical trials: clinicaltrials.gov
- Team Gleason: teamgleason.org

About the Author

JEREMY SCHREIBER was an entrepreneur, writer, and ALS warrior. He first started to write and speak about his own experiences after being diagnosed with ALS in January 2018. Drawing from his personal story, he offered a unique perspective into a world where injustice is frequent and unapologetically out in the open.

Jeremy was passionate about helping and motivating those with disabilities to improve their lives and overcome the challenges they face. He also gave a voice to the people society has rendered invisible, covering such topics as travel, new treatments, medical marijuana, and technology.

After a long, courageous battle with ALS, Jeremy passed away on October 29, 2021. His parents, Fred and Ronnye Schreiber, are proud to carry on his legacy.